Effective Carbon Rates 2018

PRICING CARBON EMISSIONS THROUGH TAXES
AND EMISSIONS TRADING

This work is published under the responsibility of the Secretary-General of the OECD. The opinions expressed and arguments employed herein do not necessarily reflect the official views of OECD member countries.

This document, as well as any data and any map included herein, are without prejudice to the status of or sovereignty over any territory, to the delimitation of international frontiers and boundaries and to the name of any territory, city or area.

Please cite this publication as:
OECD (2018), *Effective Carbon Rates 2018: Pricing Carbon Emissions Through Taxes and Emissions Trading*, OECD Publishing, Paris.
https://doi.org/10.1787/9789264305304-en

ISBN 978-92-64-30529-8 (print)
ISBN 978-92-64-30530-4 (PDF)

The statistical data for Israel are supplied by and under the responsibility of the relevant Israeli authorities. The use of such data by the OECD is without prejudice to the status of the Golan Heights, East Jerusalem and Israeli settlements in the West Bank under the terms of international law.

Photo credits: Cover © west cowboy/Shutterstock.com, ©Nivellen77/Shutterstock.com

Corrigenda to OECD publications may be found on line at: *www.oecd.org/about/publishing/corrigenda.htm*.
© OECD 2018

You can copy, download or print OECD content for your own use, and you can include excerpts from OECD publications, databases and multimedia products in your own documents, presentations, blogs, websites and teaching materials, provided that suitable acknowledgment of the source and copyright owner(s) is given. All requests for public or commercial use and translation rights should be submitted to *rights@oecd.org*. Requests for permission to photocopy portions of this material for public or commercial use shall be addressed directly to the Copyright Clearance Center (CCC) at *info@copyright.com* or the Centre francais d'exploitation du droit de copie (CFC) at *contact@cfcopies.com*.

Foreword

This report was prepared by the Tax Policy and Statistics division in the OECD's Centre for Tax Policy and Administration under the auspices of the Committee on Fiscal Affairs and the Environment Policy Committee. It is unique in its comprehensive approach, integrating carbon prices that result from taxes and emissions trading systems. It provides detailed effective carbon rates for 42 OECD and G20 countries in 2015 and 2012, as well as estimates of the effective carbon rates in 2018.

The report was drafted by Florens Flues and Kurt Van Dender. The database architecture was developed and updated by Luisa Dressler and Florens Flues. Information on emissions trading systems was collected and processed by Johanna Arlinghaus, Luisa Dressler, Florens Flues, Melanie Marten and Jonas Teusch. Carrie Tyler improved the presentation and the dissemination of the work. Michael Sharratt advised on graphical design and the implementation of new publication processes. All contributors are in the OECD's Centre for Tax Policy and Administration, in the case of Jonas Teusch through a joint appointment with the Environment Directorate.

The authors would like to thank their colleagues Nils Axel Braathen and David Bradbury from the OECD for their very insightful feedback on earlier versions of the report.

The report was discussed by the OECD's Joint Meetings of Tax and Environment Experts, and it was approved for declassification by the Committee on Fiscal Affairs and the Environment Policy Committee. The authors would like to thank in particular the delegates to the Joint Meetings and their colleagues in supranational, national and subnational government administrations for their assistance with the provision of data, as well as for invaluable suggestions, inputs and comments received at various stages of preparing the data and the report.

Table of contents

Foreword 3
Executive Summary 7
    Main findings 8
    Implications 9

Chapter 1. Introduction 11
    Notes 17
    References 17

Chapter 2. Carbon pricing trends – Reasons to be cheerful 19
    The current state of carbon pricing: a white shade of blue 22
    Carbon pricing trends: expanding coverage, persistently low rates 24
    The distribution of effective carbon rates is strongly skewed 27
    The carbon pricing gap 29
    Notes 35
    References 36

Chapter 3. Carbon pricing in 2015 – Detailed analysis 39
    Share of emissions priced and price levels across countries in 2015 40
    Carbon pricing gap across countries in 2015 54
    Carbon pricing – a bigger picture 57
    Notes 71
    References 71
    A.1. Description of emissions trading systems used in the analysis 76
    A.2. Permit prices and ETS coverage 80
    A.3. ETS-specific adjustments and assumptions 82
    Notes 88
    References 88

Tables

Table 2.1. Emissions coverage and permit price – assumptions for 2018 21
Table 2.2. Taxes dominate the composition of ECRs 27
Table 2.3. Carbon pricing gap by sector 34
Table 3.1. Proportion of emissions priced per tonne of CO_2 by country 42
Table 3.2. Emissions from electricity generation fall sharply with the introduction of a carbon price
    support 43
Table 3.3. Proportion of emissions priced in the electricity sector per tonne of CO_2 by country 45
Table 3.4. Proportion of emissions priced in the industry sector per tonne of CO_2 by country 47

Table 3.5. Proportion of emissions priced in the residential and commercial sector per tonne of CO_2 by country 49
Table 3.6. Proportion of emissions priced in the road sector per tonne of CO_2 by country 51
Table 3.7. Carbon pricing gap at EUR 30 in 2015 55
Table 3.8. Carbon pricing gap at EUR 60 in 2015 57

Annex Table 3.A.1. Proportion of emissions priced per tonne of CO_2 by country 64
Annex Table 3.A.2. Proportion of emissions priced in the electricity sector per tonne of CO_2 by country 65
Annex Table 3.A.3. Proportion of emissions priced in the industry sector per tonne of CO_2 by country 66
Annex Table 3.A.4. Proportion of emissions priced in the residential and commercial sector per tonne of CO_2 by country 67
Annex Table 3.A.5. Proportion of emissions priced in the road transport sector per tonne of CO_2 by country 68
Annex Table 3.A.6. Carbon pricing gap at EUR 30 in 2015 69
Annex Table 3.A.7. Carbon pricing gap at EUR 60 in 2015 70

Table A.1. Description of emissions trading systems used in the analysis 77
Table A.2. Permit prices and ETS coverage 81

Figures

Figure 1.1. Components of effective carbon rates 14
Figure 2.1 A cost-effective low-carbon transition requires higher carbon prices 22
Figure 2.2. Share of emissions from energy use priced above EUR 60 per tonne of CO_2 24
Figure 2.3. Estimated proportion of CO_2 emissions priced at different price levels 25
Figure 2.4 Proportion of CO_2 emission priced by sector 26
Figure 2.5. Proportion of CO_2 emissions from energy use subject to different levels of effective carbon rates in 42 OECD and G20 countries 28
Figure 2.6. The carbon pricing gap 30
Figure 3.1. Proportion of CO_2 emissions priced at different price levels in 2015 40
Figure 3.2. Estimates of marginal external costs and of fuel tax, France and United Kingdom, in EUR per litre of gasoline and diesel 53
Figure 3.3. Less populous countries have a smaller carbon pricing gap 58
Figure 3.4. Countries with a low carbon pricing gap lead in decarbonising their economies 59
Figure 3.5. Countries with a lower carbon pricing gap are more carbon efficient 60

Boxes

Box 1.1. Why carbon pricing works 13
Box 1.2. The effective carbon rate (ECR) 14
Box 2.1. The carbon pricing gap 33
Box 3.1. External costs in road transport 52

Executive Summary

Pricing carbon emissions allows countries to smoothly steer their economies towards and along a carbon-neutral growth path. By putting a price on carbon emissions, countries can increase resource efficiency, boost investment in clean energy, develop and sell low-emission goods and services, and increase resilience to risks inherent in deep structural change. Failing to price carbon emissions now, increases the risk that the planet overheats, with average temperatures increasing by five or more degrees. Adaptation to such increases might be possible, but would likely be extremely costly. Decisive action to reduce the risk is by far the better option.

Pricing carbon emissions is important for moving to carbon-neutral growth. This second edition of *Effective Carbon Rates* shows how 42 OECD and G20 countries, representing 80% of world emissions, price carbon emissions from energy use today, and how much progress has been made since 2012.

Carbon prices are measured using the *effective carbon rate* (ECR). The ECR is the sum of three components: specific taxes on fossil fuels, carbon taxes and prices of tradable emission permits. All three components increase the price of high-carbon relative to low- and zero-carbon fuels, encouraging energy users to go for low- or zero-carbon options.

In each of the 42 countries, the ECRs are measured for six economic sectors: industry, electricity generation, residential and commercial energy use, road transport, off-road transport, and agriculture and fisheries. The report discusses the change of ECRs by comparing pricing patterns in 2012, 2015 and estimates for 2018.

The *carbon pricing gap* measures the difference between actual ECRs and benchmark rates. The report considers two benchmark rates: EUR 30, a low-end estimate of carbon costs today; and EUR 60, a midpoint estimate of the carbon costs in 2020 and a low-end estimate for 2030. The carbon pricing gap indicates the extent to which polluters do not pay for the damage from carbon emissions.

The aggregate carbon pricing gap summarises the current use of market-based, cost-effective tools to decarbonise across the 42 countries studied. At the country level, a low gap can also be seen as an indicator of long-term competitiveness, i.e. being well prepared for the low-carbon economy.

In order to close the gap, it is essential to price currently unpriced emissions, either through emissions trading or tax reform. Emissions trading can be an effective option, noting that true support for low and zero-carbon investments needs higher and more stable permit prices than currently observed. Taxes have the advantage of simple administration, especially when grafted onto existing excise tax regimes. In many sectors, tax rates currently fall short of benchmarks and will need to increase significantly to reflect carbon costs. Revenue-neutral reforms allow to cut other taxes.

Main findings

While the aggregate carbon pricing gap is declining at a snail's pace, there are reasons to be cheerful

- The aggregate carbon pricing gap is declining at a snail's pace. Using EUR 30 per tonne of CO_2 as a benchmark, the gap for the 42 countries as a whole dropped from 83% in 2012 to 79.5% in 2015, and is estimated to reach 76.5% in 2018. Smooth and cost-effective decarbonisation requires the carbon pricing gap to close much faster.

- New carbon pricing initiatives have the potential to significantly reduce the carbon pricing gap. Nation-wide emissions trading in China could lead to a significant drop of the global carbon pricing gap, to 63% in the early 2020s. Canada may nearly close its national carbon pricing gap through new carbon pricing efforts by that time.

- Several countries, including France, India, Korea, Mexico, and the United Kingdom, shrank their carbon pricing gaps between 2012 and 2015. Korea implemented a national emissions trading system in 2015. France and Mexico reformed their taxes on energy use. The United Kingdom implemented a price floor for electricity sector emissions covered by the European Union Emissions Trading System. India reduced its carbon pricing gap by increasing excise duties on transport fuels.

The carbon pricing gap varies widely, both across countries and across sectors within countries

- At the country level, the carbon pricing gap ranged from 27% to 100% in 2015. A dozen of countries have carbon pricing gaps of about 40% or lower. Countries with a low gap tend to emit fewer emissions than countries that hardly price any carbon emissions. Low-gap countries also produce fewer emissions per unit of GDP.

- The carbon pricing gap varies substantially across sectors. It exceeds 80% in electricity generation, in industry and in the residential and commercial sector. The gap is lowest in road transport, at 21%.

Taxes on energy dominate the composition of effective carbon rates in all sectors except electricity generation

- In road transport, agriculture and fisheries and household and commercial energy use, well over 90% of the effective carbon rates result from taxes. The composition is different in electricity generation, where permit prices contribute more than 80% of the effective carbon rate.

Implications

Closing the carbon pricing gap helps countries prosper in a low carbon economy and increases resilience

- Countries that close the carbon pricing gap now encourage investment in clean technologies, create new markets and benefit from ever cheaper renewable power. Countries that continue to leave the gap wide open risk high dependency on increasingly uncompetitive technologies and very high transition costs.

Chapter 1. Introduction

> *This chapter provides the context and motivation for the analysis of effective carbon rates. Effective carbon rates are the total price that applies to carbon dioxide emissions from energy use as a result of market-based instruments (specific energy taxes, carbon taxes and carbon emission permit prices). The chapter also provides an overview of the main results for 42 OECD and G20 countries, which together account for about 80% of global carbon emissions from energy use.*

Clean air, pure water and moderate temperatures provide numerous benefits to individuals, companies and countries. Where these are available, people tend to be healthier, happier and more productive, and threats to biodiversity are more limited. Climate change poses a threat to these environmental and natural resources.

Global temperatures have risen by one degree Celsius above pre-industrial levels and are expected to rise further if greenhouse gas emission patterns remain as they are. In the absence of decisive policy shifts, the planet risks overheating, with average temperatures increasing by five or more degrees Celsius compared to now. Adaptation to such increases would most likely be extremely costly.

Given the upward pressure from global GDP on the demand for energy services, cutting emissions from energy use is a *conditio sine qua non* for containing the risks of climate change, and this ultimately requires shifting energy use to carbon-neutral fuels, i.e., decarbonisation. In addition, phasing out fossil fuels reduces air pollution by reducing emissions of particulate matter and other local pollutants. This also reduces water pollution as there will be less acid rain.

Failing to act increases the risk of disaster. Delaying action risks driving up the costs of shifting to carbon-neutral fuels. As power plants, boilers and other energy assets tend to be long lived, continuing to invest in carbon-intensive asset risks incurring financial losses when carbon budgets become ever tighter in the future. Decarbonisation, starting now, therefore is imperative.

By pricing carbon emissions countries can effectively steer their economies along a carbon-neutral growth path. Carbon pricing stimulates the search for energy efficiency and ultimately encourages emitters to shift away from polluting fuels and use clean fuels instead. This mitigates carbon emissions and stimulates clean investment. Increased demand for clean fuels and assets boosts innovation and opens up new markets, allowing economies to flourish and prosper. Instead of facing increasingly scarce fossil resources, countries can tap into the abundance of renewable power.

Carbon pricing is also cost effective, i.e. it maximises the emission reductions per Euro of abatement effort. Cost effectiveness is an important ingredient of full decarbonisation, as heavily relying on abatement options that are more expensive than necessary can negatively affect economic performance and reduce social support for clean investments. Carbon pricing can also raise revenue, and this adds flexibility to fiscal policy. More carbon pricing revenue allows reducing other taxes, increasing public spending, or cutting debt.

> **Box 1.1. Why carbon pricing works**
>
> **Carbon prices maximise emission reductions from each Euro invested in abatement**
>
> Pricing greenhouse gas emissions is an essential climate mitigation policy. Pricing emissions, through taxes or tradable emission permits, encourages emitters to seek cost effective abatement options. The introduction or strengthening of carbon prices also signals strong policy commitment, creating certainty for investors that it pays to invest in carbon-neutral technologies.
>
> Carbon prices are effective for reducing emissions because they increase the price of carbon-based energy, so decreasing demand for it (Arlinghaus (2015[1]); Martin et al. (2016[2])). Pricing carbon encourages substitution towards less carbon-intensive forms of energy and lowers demand for energy overall.
>
> Taking generation of electricity as an example, producers can switch from coal to natural gas, or to zero-carbon energy sources, such as solar and wind power. In addition, where market structure and regulation allow, electricity producers will pass on the increase in production costs resulting from carbon prices to consumers of electricity, in the form of higher electricity prices, and this encourages price sensitive consumers to decrease consumption. For example, firms and households may become more vigilant about turning off appliances when they are not in use or may use them less, and they can choose more efficient appliances at the time of replacement.
>
> Carbon prices are a cost effective policy tool and that this makes them particularly attractive compared to other policy options. The cost effectiveness of carbon pricing is due to three reasons:
>
> - First, emitters have an incentive to cut emissions as long as this is cheaper than paying the price, and this equalises marginal abatement costs across emitters, ensuring economy-wide cost effectiveness.
>
> - Second, carbon prices decentralise abatement decisions, thus overcoming the asymmetry of information between the government and polluters: regulators do not need to stipulate which emissions should be reduced using which technologies.
>
> - Third, they provide an ongoing incentive to cut emissions, thus stimulating innovation.
>
> *Sources:* OECD (2016, pp. 27-35[3]) and OECD (2017, pp. 189-199[4])

This report measures progress with carbon pricing across 42 OECD and G20 economies, using the *effective carbon rate* (ECR) as a measure of carbon prices. The ECR is the total price that applies to carbon dioxide emissions from energy use as a result of market-based instruments (specific energy taxes, carbon taxes and carbon emission permit prices). The report uses the terms "carbon price" and "effective carbon rate" interchangeably. In each of the 42 countries, the ECRs are measured separately for six economic sectors: road transport, off-road transport, agriculture and fisheries, residential and commercial energy use, industry, and electricity generation.

> **Box 1.2. The effective carbon rate (ECR)**
>
> *Effective carbon rates are the total price that applies to CO_2 emissions from energy use* as a result of market-based policy instruments. They are the sum of taxes and tradable emission permit prices, and have three components (Figure 1.1):
>
> - carbon taxes, which typically set a tax rate on energy based on its carbon content,
> - specific taxes on energy use (primarily excise taxes), which are typically set per physical unit or unit of energy, but which can be translated into effective tax rates based on the carbon content of each form of energy, and
> - the price of tradable emission permits, regardless of the permit allocation method, representing the opportunity cost of emitting an extra unit of CO_2.
>
> The effective carbon rate measures how policies change the *relative* price of CO_2 emissions from energy use.
>
> **Figure 1.1. Components of effective carbon rates** 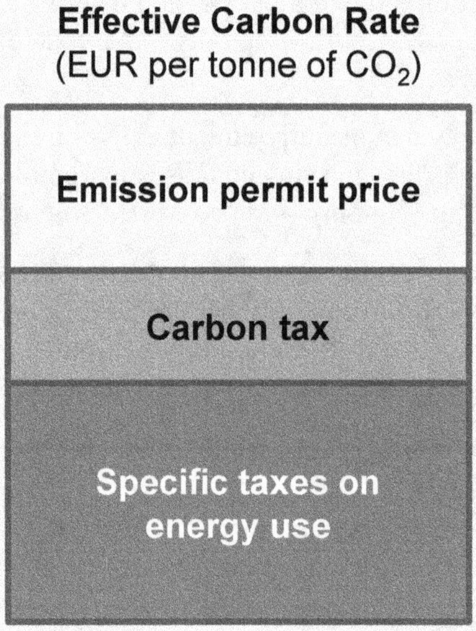
>
> **Effective Carbon Rate**
> (EUR per tonne of CO_2)
>
> - Emission permit price
> - Carbon tax
> - Specific taxes on energy use
>
> Source: OECD (2016[3]).

The report discusses the change of ECRs by comparing pricing patterns in 2012, 2015 and estimates for 2018. It discusses the distribution of the rates, and considers the "carbon pricing gap", a summary measure of the difference between actual and benchmark rates. Two benchmark values are used, EUR 30 and EUR 60 per tonne of CO_2. The first, EUR 30, is a low-end estimate of the damage that carbon emissions currently cause. Pricing emissions above EUR 30 does not guarantee that polluters pay for the full damage they cause, or that prices are sufficiently high to decarbonise economies. A price below EUR 30 does mean, however, that emitters are not directly confronted with the cost of emissions to society and that incentives for cost effective abatement are too weak.

The second benchmark, EUR 60 per tonne of CO_2, is a midpoint estimate of carbon costs in 2020, as well as a forward-looking low-end estimate of carbon costs in 2030. Rising benchmark values over time for carbon costs reflect that the marginal damage caused by one tonne of CO_2 increases with the accumulation of CO_2 in the atmosphere. Integrated assessment models show carbon prices that increase significantly in real terms over time. On the basis of such models, The High Level Commission on Carbon Pricing (2017[5]) finds that carbon prices should amount to *at least* USD 40 - 80 per tonne of CO_2 by 2020 and USD 50 - 100 per tonne of CO_2 by 2030, to be able to reach the goals of the Paris Agreement.[1] These are conservative estimates in the sense that many models suggest higher price targets, and that models commonly assume that carbon prices are introduced in a context where policies are well aligned with climate objectives.

The carbon pricing gap measures the extent to which current prices fall short of a benchmark value, as a percentage. The results show that the carbon pricing gap is large, but that it falls over time. Using EUR 30 per tonne of CO_2 as the benchmark, it drops from 83% in 2012 to 79.5% in 2015, and to 76.5% in 2018. This amounts to a decline of about one percentage point per year.

While the direction of change of the carbon pricing gap is encouraging in that it indicates better use of market-based instruments to reduce CO_2 emissions, the current rate of change is too slow compared to the ambition of the Paris Agreement. This report takes the view that carbon pricing is instrumental to a cost-effective transition to a carbon-neutral economy, and that delaying decarbonisation or relying only on other policies will drive up costs, which ultimately can erode public support for ambitious climate policy. Progress with carbon pricing therefore needs to accelerate.

A close look at the drivers of the observed narrowing of the carbon pricing gap suggests that the momentum for carbon pricing in the global economy is in fact strengthening. The more countries pursue robust carbon pricing policies the stronger becomes the incentive for other countries to follow suit, creating a self-reinforcing feedback loop. The perception of carbon pricing is shifting from its role as an instrument for marginal emissions abatement, to be used sparingly and only in as far as short-term competitiveness and equity considerations allow, to its function as the keystone of the policies needed to drive a low-carbon transition.

The Paris Agreement leaves no doubt as to the objective of climate policy, namely to decarbonise economies in the course of the second half of the century. In this context, carbon pricing is pro-competitive as it prepares companies for strong performance in a low-carbon economy. Furthermore, carbon pricing engenders co-benefits, for example through reduced air pollution from energy use, and these benefits are of prime domestic importance in many countries. In addition, there is rising awareness that increased use of carbon pricing increases the flexibility of the fiscal policy toolkit, allowing modification of tax and spending policies in line with country-specific priorities.

The emergence of positive feedback loops ultimately is not a matter of policy principles or perceptions, but of policy practice. In this context, it is encouraging to note that, to a considerable degree, the narrowing of the carbon pricing gap is the consequence of broader coverage of emissions by a pricing system in relatively large and emission-intensive countries. The anticipated introduction of a country-wide emissions trading system in China and of the backstop carbon pricing policy in Canada are estimated to result in a ten percentage point increase in coverage of global CO_2 emissions by a carbon price, from 43% to 53% between 2015 and 2018. Policy action in Mexico and at the subnational level in the United States also contributed significantly to the narrowing of the carbon pricing gap. These developments contribute to a stronger worldwide carbon pricing momentum because they weaken concerns over short-run competitiveness threats and because they illustrate that growth-oriented economic policy and effective climate policy can go hand in hand.

Emissions trading systems contribute strongly to broadening coverage of emissions by a price. However, prices in these systems have not increased strongly over time, and they remain very low. This highlights the need for gradual tightening of emission caps, in line with the decarbonisation trajectories required by the Paris Agreement.

Among the recent and expected developments that bolster support for carbon pricing are the reforms of the European Union's Emissions Trading System. Future efforts to tighten the cap could drive up prices to EUR 30 or more, and this would reduce the global carbon pricing gap by three percentage points. If China follows through on its intention to extend coverage of the country-wide emissions trading system to industry, and if prices would evolve to levels above EUR 30 per tonne CO_2 (Rathi, Akshat and Huang, 2018[6]), the global carbon pricing gap would decline from 76.5% to 63%.

Persistently low price levels in emissions trading systems imply little change over time to the very high share of carbon price signals that comes from taxes, in particular taxes on energy use (and not carbon taxes). Well over 90% of the effective carbon rate in transport, agriculture and fisheries, and household and commercial use comes from taxes. In industry, the share is about two thirds. In the electricity sector, emissions trading systems dominate as taxes represent just 19% of the total price.

Higher carbon prices will lead to higher carbon pricing revenues in the short to medium term. Judicious and transparent deployment of these revenues is as important to the economic effectiveness of and public support for carbon pricing. Climate policy becomes increasingly intertwined with mainstream economic policy, and through its revenue impacts, with fiscal policy.

The effective carbon rate analysis considers all emissions trading systems and taxes on energy use in each of the 42 countries covered. However, it does not take into account support measures for fossil fuel use that may affect the carbon price, except for tax incentives delivered through energy taxes.

The OECD's database of budgetary support and tax expenditures, discussed in the *OECD Companion to the Inventory of Support Measures for Fossil Fuels 2018* (OECD, 2018[7]) identifies and documents about 1000 individual policies that support the production or consumption of fossil fuels in OECD and selected partner economies. The inventory includes direct budgetary transfers and tax expenditures that provide a benefit for fossil fuel production or consumption when compared to alternatives. Many of these tax expenditures are included in the *Taxing Energy Use* database (OECD, 2018[8]) and therefore are reflected in the tax rates used for the calculation of effective carbon rates.

Value-added taxes (VAT) affect end-user prices of energy products in many jurisdictions in addition to the three components of ECRs. VAT is usually not specific to energy products: as long as the same rate applies, the relative prices of energy products remain unchanged. In this case, VAT should not be taken into account, as effective carbon rates measure policies that change relative prices. Differential VAT rates, however, do change the relative prices of energy products and VAT then becomes a *de facto* specific tax measure. OECD (2015[9]) provides an overview of the differential VAT rates that apply in the analysed countries. Seventeen countries apply reduced or zero VAT rates on selected energy products. This counteracts the intention to increase the relative end-user prices of energy products, and can mitigate or even offset the effective carbon rate, depending on the relative magnitude of the amount of price differentiation introduced by the differential VAT rate and the effective carbon rate.

The caveats about support measures and the potential impact of VAT notwithstanding, the ECRs capture an important component – and in most of the 42 countries analysed, by far the dominant component – of policy-driven carbon pricing.

In line with previous editions of *Taxing Energy Use* (OECD (2013[10]), OECD (2015[9]) and OECD (2018[8])) as well as of *Effective Carbon Rates* (OECD, 2016[3]) this publication reports results including emissions from the *combustion* of biomass. Annex 3.A discusses the implications of the *combustion approach* and considers recent evidence on *lifecycle* emissions of biofuels. It also discusses why emission bases from *Taxing Energy Use* and *Effective Carbon Rates* are not directly comparable with UNFCCC inventories. In addition, the annex provides tables with results excluding emissions from the combustion of biomass. Readers can use these tables to draw inferences on how results change given specific information about the lifecycle emissions from biofuels.

The remainder of this report will look at the current state of carbon pricing (Chapter 2) as well as compare carbon pricing developments between 2012 and 2015 (Chapter 3).

Notes

[1] This report assumes parity of the United States Dollar and the Euro in the long term.

References

Arlinghaus, J. (2015), "Impacts of Carbon Prices on Indicators of Competitiveness: A Review of Empirical Findings", *OECD Environment Working Papers*, No. 87, OECD Publishing, Paris, http://dx.doi.org/10.1787/5js37p21grzq-en. [1]

High-Level Commission on Carbon Prices (2017), *Report of the High-Level Commission on Carbon Prices*, World Bank, Washington, D.C., https://static1.squarespace.com/static/54ff9c5ce4b0a53decccfb4c/t/59b7f2409f8dce5316811916/1505227332748/CarbonPricing_FullReport.pdf (accessed on 16 February 2018). [5]

Martin, R., M. Muûls and U. Wagner (2016), "The Impact of the European Union Emissions Trading Scheme on Regulated Firms: What Is the Evidence after Ten Years?", *Review of Environmental Economics and Policy*, Vol. 10/1, pp. 129-148, http://dx.doi.org/10.1093/reep/rev016. [2]

OECD (2018), *OECD Companion to the Inventory of Support Measures for Fossil Fuels 2018*, OECD Publishing, Paris, http://dx.doi.org/10.1787/9789264286061-en. [7]

OECD (2018), *Taxing Energy Use 2018: Companion to the Taxing Energy Use Database*, OECD Publishing, Paris. [8]

OECD (2017), *Investing in Climate, Investing in Growth*, OECD Publishing, Paris, http://dx.doi.org/10.1787/9789264273528-en. [4]

OECD (2016), *Effective Carbon Rates: Pricing CO2 through Taxes and Emissions Trading Systems*, OECD Publishing, Paris, http://dx.doi.org/10.1787/9789264260115-en. [3]

OECD (2015), *Taxing Energy Use 2015: OECD and Selected Partner Economies*, OECD Publishing, Paris, http://dx.doi.org/10.1787/9789264232334-en. [9]

OECD (2013), *Taxing Energy Use: A Graphical Analysis*, OECD Publishing, Paris, http://dx.doi.org/10.1787/9789264183933-en. [10]

Rathi, Akshat and Huang, E. (2018), *The complete guide to the world's largest carbon market that just launched in China*. [6]

Chapter 2. Carbon pricing trends – Reasons to be cheerful

This chapter describes the present state of carbon pricing and evaluates recent and ongoing developments. The gap between the minimum carbon prices that are needed to reach the targets of the Paris Agreement and those currently observed remains large and is only declining slowly. Nevertheless, there are signs that carbon pricing is gaining momentum.

This chapter presents estimates of how 42 OECD and G20 countries price carbon emissions from fuel combustion in 2018. Together, these 42 countries emit approximately 80% of global carbon emissions from fuel combustion; they also account for nearly 80% of global energy use (OECD, 2018[1]).

In order to arrive at an estimate for the state of carbon pricing in 2018, the estimates update detailed information on carbon emissions, energy taxes, carbon taxes and emissions trading systems (ETSs) in 2015 with information on recent developments in emissions trading systems, including expected developments in Canada and in China.

Table 2.1 lists, for each country with an emissions trading system, the assumed (at the time of writing this report) coverage of emissions and the price levels within the trading system. Coverage and price levels generally reflect the status of trading systems in 2018, but for China and Canada, the assumptions are forward looking in order to include the new national Chinese ETS and the carbon pricing backstop in Canada.

Table 2.1. Emissions coverage and permit price – assumptions for 2018

	Coverage	Permit Price
Canadian carbon pricing systems	New ETS in Ontario; Carbon levy and output-based systems for large polluters in Alberta; Federal backstop (consisting of a carbon charge and an output-based system for large polluters) in whole or in part in any province or territory that does not have a carbon pricing system that meets the benchmark (compliance required by 2018, implementation foreseen for 2019).	The federal benchmark requires a minimum carbon price of CAD10 (about EUR 7.50) for 2018, which increases by CAD 10 a year until reaching CAD 50 (EUR 40) in 2022. Assuming compliance by all provinces and territories, average carbon prices are expected to range between CAD 19 and CAD 23.5 in 2018, depending on sector.
Chinese ETS	National ETS covers 3 billion tonnes of CO_2 in the electricity sector in addition to emissions that have already been covered by the Chinese pilot systems; Coverage of Chinese pilot systems as in 2015	CNY 50 (about EUR 7.25) for electricity sector; CNY 11.39 (EUR 1.65) on average for the remaining sectors covered by the pilot systems
EU ETS	Same as 2015	EUR 7.60
Swiss ETS	Same as 2015	CHF 10.95 (about EUR 10.25)
Japanese ETS	Same as 2015	JPY 1320 (about EUR 9.75)
Korean ETS	Same as 2015	KRW 22000 (about EUR 17.60)
New Zealand ETS	Same as 2015	NZD 5.63 (about EUR 3.55)
ETS in the USA	Two additional systems are included: The Washington Clean Air Rule covers about 50 million tonnes of CO_2 from energy use; The Massachusetts ETS on emissions in the power sector covers about 9 million tonnes of CO_2 from energy use; Coverage for California and RGGI system as in 2015	USD 7.74 (about EUR 7.00) on average for the electricity sector, USD 14.67 (EUR 13.25) on average for industry and USD 14.89 (EUR 13.45) on average for all other sectors

Note: See the Annex for further detail.

Some countries have increased energy and carbon taxes since 2015 (OECD, 2017[2]), but data limitations prevent these changes from being considered here. The tax data used in this chapter are for 2015, because the process of collecting and allocating new tax rates to emissions is too time consuming to allow for quick updating. While these changes can have a significant effect on the share and level of priced emissions at the country level, their impact on the overall level and share of emission prices is likely to be limited. Nevertheless, the use of 2015 tax data implies that this chapter likely shows lower-end estimates of effective carbon rates for 2018.

The analysis combines the price information for 2018 with 2015 emissions data. Detailed data on carbon emissions from energy use are available only with a substantial time lag. The latest year for which detailed data was available at the time of production of this report is 2015. However, emission levels change generally only by a few percentage points a year at most, so that data from 2015 is still informative for emission levels in 2018.

Overall, the estimate for 2018 is detailed in its treatment of sectors and carbon pricing instruments. It accounts for recent developments, and for some expected developments, in emissions trading, while relying on 2015 data for taxes and for energy use.

The current state of carbon pricing: a white shade of blue

Figure 2.1 summarises the current state of carbon pricing at the country level. The darker the shade of blue, the higher the share of emissions from fossil fuel combustion that is subject to an effective carbon rate of at least EUR 30 per tonne of CO_2. EUR 30 is a low-end estimate of the damage that carbon emissions cause to society. Pricing emissions below EUR 30 means that emitters are not directly confronted with the full cost of emissions to society and that incentives for cost-effective abatement are too weak.

The map is predominantly pale blue fading to white. This shows that currently few countries price a significant share of their emissions above EUR 30 per tonne CO_2.

Figure 2.1 A cost-effective low-carbon transition requires higher carbon prices

Share of emissions from energy use priced above EUR 30 per tonne of CO_2, estimate for 2018

No country prices all emissions at EUR 30 per tonne of CO_2 or above, but several European countries price more than half of their emissions at or above this level (Figure 2.1). If the permit price in the EU ETS was to increase to EUR 30, e.g. through the introduction of a minimum price like in the United Kingdom or through a significantly faster decline of the aggregate emission cap, 68% of aggregate emissions from all EU countries covered in the study would be priced above EUR 30, compared to 31% today. Eight European countries would price more than three quarters of their emission above EUR 30: The Netherlands, Norway, Greece, Spain, Italy, Luxembourg, Ireland and Slovenia. The significant increase in the share of emissions priced above EUR 30 says that the coverage of the ETS is fairly broad, so that higher prices strongly affect effective carbon rates in Europe. As will be seen, this is the case particularly in the electricity sector and in industry.

In the African, American, Asian and Oceanian countries covered in the study, only small shares of CO_2 emissions are priced above EUR 30 per tonne. Mexico reaches the highest share in the Americas, with about 30% of emissions priced at or above this level. The national ETS in China substantially changes the share of emissions covered, but initial permit prices are expected to be below EUR 30, so that the share of emissions priced at EUR 30 or more remains below 20%. The section on the "carbon pricing gap" will discuss the impacts of the Chinese national ETS in more detail.

The marginal damage caused by one tonne of CO_2 increases with the accumulation of CO_2 in the atmosphere. Accordingly, integrated assessment models show carbon prices that increase significantly in real terms over time. On the basis of such models, the High Level Commission on Carbon Pricing (2017[3]) finds that carbon prices should amount to at least USD 40 – 80 per tonne of CO_2 by 2020 and USD 50 – 100 per tonne of CO_2 by 2030, to be able to reach the goals of the Paris Agreement.

In line with the estimates of the High Level Commission on Carbon Pricing (2017[3]), this report adopts EUR 60 as a second benchmark:[1] EUR 60 is the midpoint estimate of carbon costs in 2020 and a low-end estimate of carbon costs in 2030.

Figure 2.2. Share of emissions from energy use priced above EUR 60 per tonne of CO_2

Figure 2.2 shows the percentage of emissions priced at EUR 60 per tonne of CO_2 or more, by country. It is clear that all countries need to raise carbon prices soon and significantly to reach the goals of the Paris Agreement. Currently, only three countries price more than 40% of their emissions above EUR 60 per tonne CO_2, namely Luxembourg, Norway and Slovenia. Most of these emissions are from road transport. Emissions from other sectors are priced at significantly lower rates, or not all, as will be discussed in the coming paragraphs. In the Americas, Mexico is the only country that prices more than 30% of its emissions above EUR 60.

Carbon pricing trends: expanding coverage, persistently low rates

Figure 2.3 shows that in 2018, 54% of CO_2 emissions from fuel combustion are estimated to be subject to a positive carbon price, across all the 42 OECD and G20 countries covered in this report. This is 10 percentage points more than in 2015. The Chinese national ETS and carbon pricing in Canada drive this development. Subnational emissions trading systems in the United States have also contributed to the increase in coverage of emissions by a carbon pricing system.

Figure 2.3. Estimated proportion of CO$_2$ emissions priced at different price levels

Price levels in EUR per tonne of CO$_2$

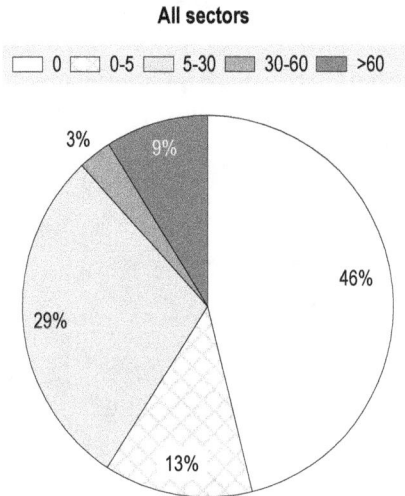

While the overall share of priced emissions has increased significantly, price levels remain low. By the estimates for 2018, 13% of emissions face a price between EUR 0 and 5, and 29% are priced between EUR 5 and 30 per tonne CO$_2$. Only 12% of emissions face a price above EUR 30 – this is the same share as in 2015; the share of emissions priced above EUR 60 has also remained stable at 9%.

In sectors other than road transport and electricity generation, few emissions are subject to a price

Figure 2.4 shows that price coverage and price levels differ strongly across sectors. In the road transport sector, which accounts for 16% of total emissions, 97% of emissions are priced. Fifty-seven percent face an effective carbon rate above EUR 30, and 48% a rate above EUR 60, per tonne of CO$_2$. In short, emissions from the road transport sector face significantly stronger carbon rates than emissions from other sectors

Figure 2.4 Proportion of CO₂ emission priced by sector

Price levels in EUR per tonne of CO_2

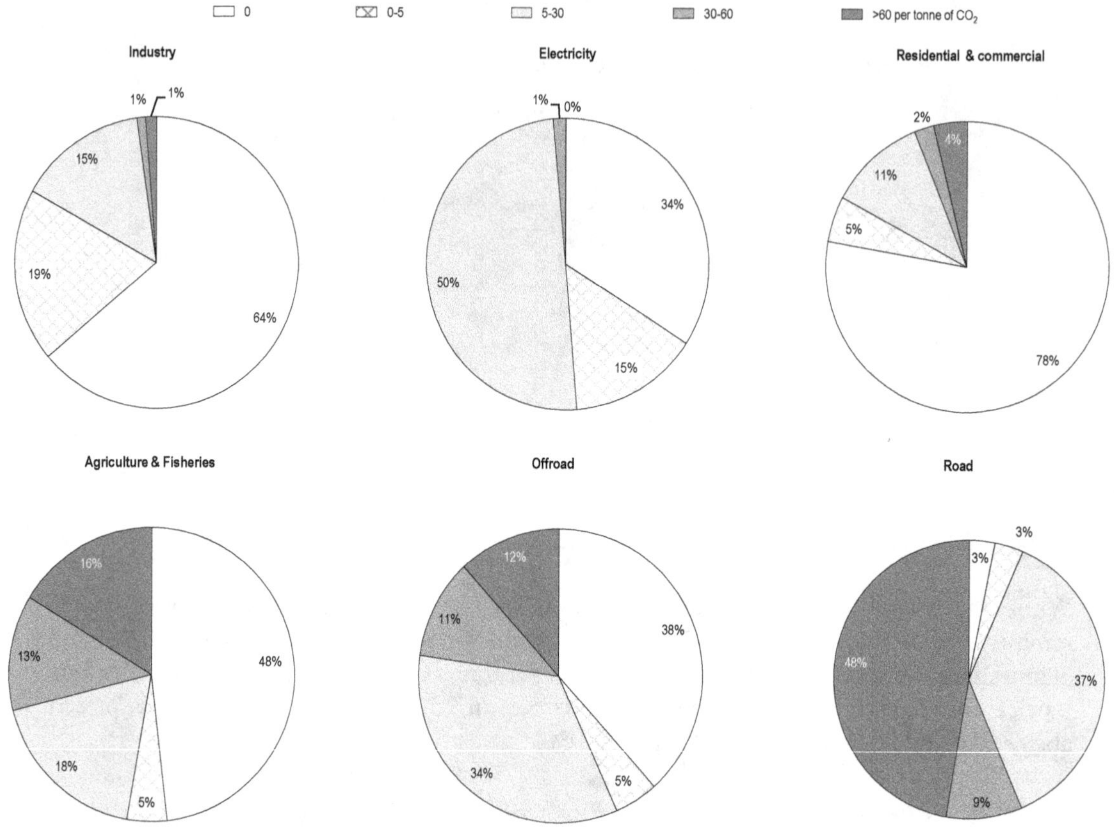

Legend: 0 | 0-5 | 5-30 | 30-60 | >60 per tonne of CO_2

Industry: 64%, 19%, 15%, 1%, 1%

Electricity: 0%, 15%, 50%, 34%, 1%

Residential & commercial: 78%, 5%, 11%, 4%, 2%

Agriculture & Fisheries: 48%, 5%, 18%, 13%, 16%

Offroad: 38%, 5%, 34%, 11%, 12%

Road: 3%, 37%, 9%, 48%, 3%

The electricity sector accounts for 31% of total CO_2 emissions from fuel combustion. Two-thirds of these emissions face a positive effective carbon rate. In 2015, this share was only one third – the Chinese national ETS has strongly expanded carbon pricing coverage in the electricity sector.

For 15% of emissions from the electricity sector, the carbon rate is below EUR 5 per tonne of CO_2. Half of the emissions face a carbon rate between EUR 5 and 30. The effective carbon rate is above EUR 30 for only 1% of emissions.

In the industry sector, the source of more than a third of total emissions from fossil fuel combustion, about two-thirds of emissions are unpriced. Price levels remain low for the remaining third of industrial emissions. Only 2% of emissions are priced above EUR 30. Furthermore, compared to 2015, there has hardly been any change.

In the residential and commercial sector 78% of emissions are not subject to a carbon price. Sixteen percent are priced between EUR 0 and EUR 30 per tonne of CO_2, and 6% above EUR 30. Carbon price coverage and price levels have also remained stable between 2015 and 2018. The residential and commercial sector accounts for 13% of total emissions.

About half of emissions in the agriculture and fisheries sectors face a positive price, and nearly 30% of emissions are priced above EUR 30. In the offroad transport sector, 38% of emissions are unpriced, while 18% face a price of at least EUR 30 per tonne CO_2.[2] Relatively high effective carbon rates in these sectors are due to relatively high tax rates for oil products used in these sectors. Compared to 2015, few changes are observed. The agriculture and fisheries sector contributes 1%, and the non-road sector 2%, to total emissions.

Taxes dominate the composition of effective carbon rates

In most sectors taxes clearly are the largest component of effective carbon rates, see Table 2.2. Over 93% of the overall carbon price signal stems from taxes in the agriculture and fisheries sector, the road and offroad transport sectors and in the residential and commercial sector. Permit prices from emission trading systems contribute significantly to the effective carbon rates in the industry sector, but across the 42 countries, 62% of the effective carbon rate nevertheless results from taxes.

Table 2.2. Taxes dominate the composition of ECRs

Sector	Share of tax component in total ECR
Agriculture & fisheries	98%
Electricity	19%
Industry	62%
Offroad transport	96%
Residential and commercial	93%
Road transport	99%

In the electricity sector, emissions trading systems drive carbon pricing efforts. Permit prices are by far the largest component of the ECR, at 81% across the 42 countries. As discussed, coverage is broad and expanding, but price levels remain low.

The distribution of effective carbon rates is strongly skewed

Figure 2.5 shows the cumulative distribution of effective carbon rates for all 42 OECD and G20 countries combined. The distribution is skewed to the right, i.e. a small share of emissions face a high effective carbon rate, while many emissions face no or a very low rate. This shape has implications for the interpretation of evidence on effective carbon rates, as the following paragraphs explain.

Figure 2.5. Proportion of CO_2 emissions from energy use subject to different levels of effective carbon rates in 42 OECD and G20 countries

Estimate for 2018

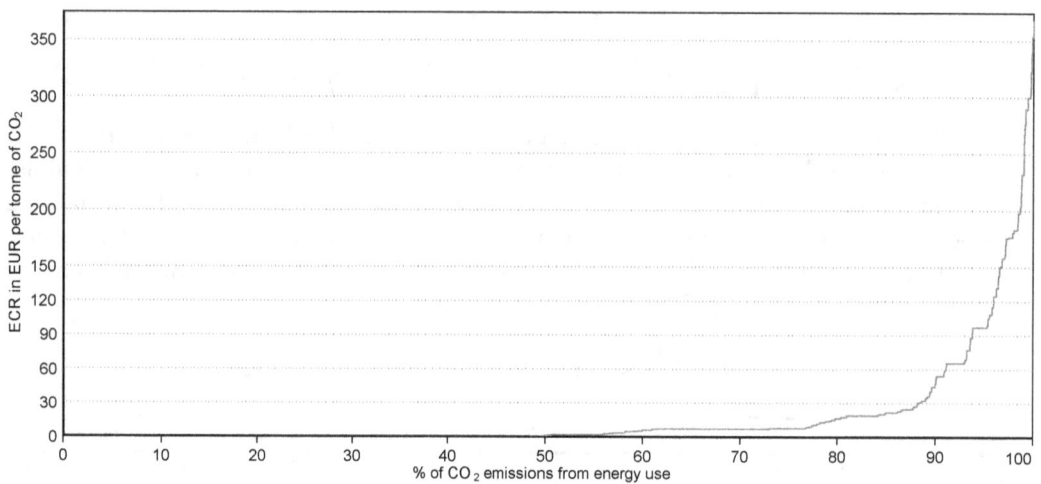

First, average effective carbon rates provide little information about the state of carbon pricing within a country. Average carbon rates would be relatively high, as the few emissions that face a high carbon rate strongly impact the calculation of average rates. For example, if country A charges an effective rate of EUR 2.5 for 90% of emissions and of EUR 227.5 for 10% of emissions, the average rate is EUR 25 per tonne, but this price is very different from what applies to any given tonne of emissions in country A. In practice, average rates hide the reality that the vast majority of emissions face prices near or equal to zero.[3]

Relying on average rates can also muddy the waters for intercountry comparisons. Assume, for example, that country B charges a uniform rate of EUR 25 per tonne for all CO_2 emissions from combustion. The average rate then is the same as in country A above, but the actual rate pattern is very different.

Second, for making statements about the polluter-pays principle, i.e. to what extent polluters pay for the damage their emissions cause to society, the share of emissions priced above and below the social cost estimate needs to be known. Comparing average carbon rates to social cost estimates does not allow any systematic assessment of how far the polluter-pays principle is implemented. As average carbon rates are strongly influenced by the small share of highly priced emissions, see Figure 2.5, comparisons would be misleading.

Third, average effective carbon rates allow no appreciation of the cost effectiveness of carbon abatement.[4,5] If some emitters face no or a very low carbon price, while other emitters face a very high carbon price, abatement will not be cost effective (as in country A above, in contrast to country B which applies a uniform rate). Emitters with a high price undertake expensive abatement options while those with no carbon price forego low-cost abatement opportunities. Average rates do not allow for an appreciation of whether any two emitters face the same or a different carbon price, only the average carbon price for both of them is visible. Hence, inferences about the cost effectiveness of abatement that can be drawn using average carbon are limited.

For the reasons mentioned above, this publication shows either the full distribution of effective carbon rates as in Figure 2.5, or pie charts that summarise the distribution at several benchmark values, or at the very least breaks down averages by sector. For example, Figure 2.3 on page 25 summarises Figure 2.4 by showing that 47% of emissions are unpriced, 89% of emissions are priced below EUR 30 and 91% of emissions have an effective carbon rate below EUR 60.

The carbon pricing gap

The *carbon pricing gap* is a summary indicator of countries' use of carbon pricing. It compares the distribution of actual effective carbon rates to a benchmark rate. This report uses two benchmark values, EUR 30 and EUR 60 per tonne of CO_2. The first is a low-end estimate of the carbon costs today, the second a midpoint estimate of carbon costs in 2020, as well as a forward looking low-end estimate of carbon costs in 2030. This section discusses the structure of the indicator, how it can be interpreted, and how it can be reduced.

The carbon pricing summarises the state of carbon pricing

The carbon pricing gap shows the extent to which countries price carbon emissions below the benchmark value, by measuring the difference between the benchmark and the actual rate for every percentile, and summing all positive differences. The gap is measured as a percentage. If the ECR on all emissions was at least as high as the benchmark value, the gap would be zero, and if the ECR was zero throughout, the gap would be 100%.

The carbon pricing gap can be calculated at the level of countries or across aggregates of all or groups of countries. Within these groups, it can be considered across all economic sectors, or at the level of individual sectors. This report considers the carbon pricing gap across all countries and sectors, and presents country level and sector level estimates across countries.

The aggregate carbon pricing gap indicates how advanced the 42 countries are with the implementation of market-based, cost-effective tools to decarbonise their economies. The measure describes the state of carbon pricing, and can be tracked across time and compared across companies and sectors (noting that higher prices in transport are common, and are not directly indicative of sufficiently high fuel prices, given the presence of other external costs). It can also be seen as indicative of countries' effort, through cost-effective policies, to reduce CO_2 emissions from energy use.

The carbon pricing gap considers only market-based policies, not the full spectrum of measures, and in that sense does not capture all climate policy effort related to energy use. A high gap suggests limited overall effort or, given that alternative policies are very likely more costly, effort at relatively high costs. Given commitments to decarbonisation, it therefore is interpretable of the risk countries are subject to by not focussing on cost-effective decarbonisation. At the country level, the gap also can be seen as an indicator of long-run competitiveness. This is discussed in the next subsection.

The carbon pricing gap is a better summary measure than the average effective carbon rate because it is sensitive to the distribution of the rates, but not heavily influenced by extreme values. Consider the example of the previous section, where country A charges an effective rate of EUR 2.5 for 90% of emissions and of EUR 227.5 for 10% of emissions (leading to an average rate of EUR 25 per tonne), and country B applies a uniform rate of EUR 25. The carbon pricing gap against a EUR 30 benchmark in country

A is 82.5% (reflecting the large gap between actual rates and the benchmark for 90% of emissions) and is much lower, at 16.7%. in country B (because all emissions are priced at a rate close to the benchmark). That said, the carbon pricing gap does not capture the full characteristics of the shape of the distribution, and it can be equal across countries that in fact have differing carbon pricing patterns. For example, the carbon pricing gap is 50% in a country that charges zero rates for half its emissions and rates above EUR 30 for the other half, and it will be 50% in a country that charges EUR 15 per tonne for all emissions.

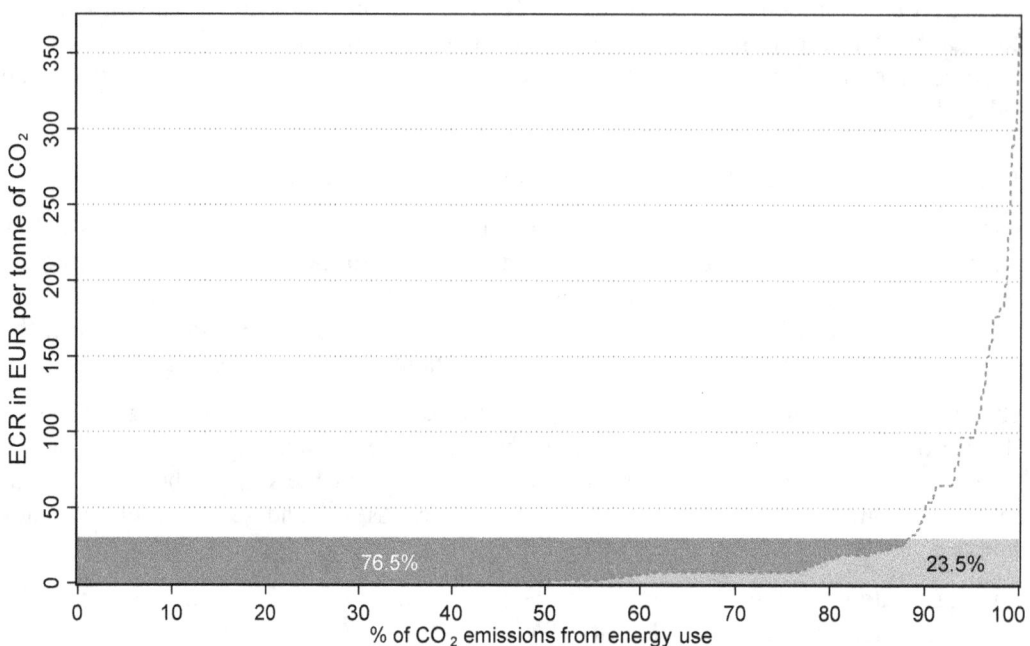

Figure 2.6. The carbon pricing gap

Shown in dark blue

Note: Estimate for 2018.

Figure 2.6 illustrates the *carbon pricing gap against a EUR 30 benchmark* for effective carbon rate estimates for 2018. The dashed line shows the distribution of carbon rates across the 42 economies as a whole, the same as in Figure 2.5. The proportion of emissions below the dashed line is subject to a positive carbon rate (coloured light blue). The proportion of emissions between the dashed line and the horizontal line at EUR 30 per tonne of CO_2 (coloured dark blue) is either not priced by any price instrument, or is priced at a level below EUR 30 per tonne of CO_2. The area in dark blue is the *carbon pricing gap* across the 42 countries today, and it equals 76.5%.

The *carbon pricing gap at EUR 60* is 83%.

The carbon pricing gap as an indicator of long-term competitiveness

With the Paris Agreement, countries decided to decarbonise their economies by the mid to end of this century. Given this commitment, strategic incentives are now in favour of comprehensive and significant carbon prices. Carbon prices are the most cost-effective tool to reduce emissions, (see page 11 and OECD, 2016[1], Chapter 2 for an in-depth explanation). This means that countries with few emissions priced or with low effective carbon rates pay too much for abatement today or that they delay abatement. Delaying abatement until it is unavoidable severely risks increasing the costs, since carbon-intensive capital can suddenly become obsolete (European Systemic Risk Board, 2016[4]).

Against this background, the *carbon pricing gap* can be seen as an indicator of long-term competitiveness during the low-carbon transition. A low or zero gap signals to investors that a country seeks to decarbonise at lowest cost and that its companies are being incentivised to compete and thrive in a low-carbon economy. A high gap indicates either of two undesirable states of the economy, excessively costly effort or low effort, as explained in the following paragraphs.

First, a high gap can signal that a country spends too much money on abatement. Relying mainly or only on non-price mitigation policies means that firms and households spend more or invest less, or that the government runs higher deficits, for the same level of abatement compared to the case where it had priced carbon emissions. This risks lowering economic growth and, more broadly, welfare, as resources are allocated inefficiently. Pursuing mitigation policies in a way that is more costly than necessary can increase sovereign risk and reduce productive potential. Given the size of effort required to become fully carbon neutral in the second half the century, these risks are considerable.

Second, a high gap can reflect a country's limited effort towards a low-carbon economy. Firms are then more likely to forego the opportunities that arise in a low-carbon economy and face higher transition risks. In addition, the country's overall economy is more likely to face economic adversity and become less competitive due to lack of climate policy or late action.

Foregone opportunities include not increasing resource efficiency, not taking advantage of ever-cheaper clean energy, missing out on developing and selling low-emission goods and services, not being present in emerging low-carbon markets and not becoming more resilient to climate shocks (TCFD, 2017[5]). This likely diminishes long term growth, even if such an approach can lead to short run gains. Aiming to take advantage of the low-carbon transition, ever more companies are adopting in-house carbon pricing systems and are procuring low-carbon energy (Ceres (2017[6]), Kersting and Stratmann (2018[7])).

Transition risks consist of technology risks, market risks, reputation risks, litigation and policy risks (TCFD (2017[5]);). Technology risks arise when new low-carbon technologies become cheaper than traditional high-carbon technologies. The value of high-carbon assets can then suddenly drop. Market risks refer to changes in customer preferences (from existing high-carbon to new low-carbon products and services) and the possibility of increased raw material prices (through ever more difficult access or stricter regulation). Reputation risks include increased negative stakeholder feedback as well as the stigmatisation of carbon-intensive firms and sectors.

Hunt et al. (2017[8]) argue that fossil fuel disinvestment campaigns already increased investor's awareness of climate change risks, while it is too early to say how much disinvestment and asset devaluation this has caused. Litigation risks cover cases of loss and damage brought forward against highly polluting firms as well as citizens suing to hold their governments accountable for climate commitments (see UNEP (2017[9]) and Nachmany et al. (2017[10]) for recent reviews). Policy risk refers to unexpected measure of stricter greenhouse gas regulation, for example in response to extreme climate events (Zenghelis and Stern, 2016[11]).

If a transition risk materialises, this can suddenly decrease the value of high-carbon assets considerably, possibly triggering a "Climate Minsky moment". Bank of England Governor Mark Carney describes a Climate Minsky moment as a situation where for a long time investors are insufficiently taking account of transition risks and ultimately find the cost of adjusting to the low-carbon economy to be higher than expected (Shankleman and Lacqua, 2017[12]).[6] Such sudden and elevated adaptation costs have the potential to trigger a severe economic crisis.

Carbon pricing mechanisms help prevent Climate Minsky moments and the *carbon pricing gap* shows the extent to which countries are utilising them. Carbon prices encourage cost-effective climate change mitigation by ensuring that all economic actors take the costs of emissions into account in their business and investment decisions. Carbon prices make it more costly to sustain the behavioural bias of ignoring the low-carbon transition. Increasing carbon prices gradually allows asset prices to adjust smoothly and reduce the risk of high economic costs following a sudden devaluation of carbon-intensive assets.

How countries can reduce the carbon pricing gap

Compared to 2015, the current carbon pricing gap at EUR 30 across all 42 OECD and G20 countries decreased by 3 percentage point, from 79.5% to 76.5%. In 2012, the gap was more than 6 percentage points higher, at 83%. While the gap is narrowing, the process is slow. If the decrease was to continue by 1 percentage point a year, the gap would close by 2095. This means that carbon prices need to increase considerably more quickly than they have done in recent years in order to ensure a cost-effective low-carbon transition.

While aggregate progress has been slow, current and planned actions by individual countries can lead to a substantial decline. The expected development of the Chinese ETS is an example. In addition to covering electricity generation in its national ETS (NDRC, 2017[13]), China announced its intention to include industry emissions. Carbon market experts expect low permit prices around Yuan 50 per tonne of CO_2 (about EUR 6.4) for the start of the national ETS, but substantial price increases to about Yuan 200-300 (EUR 25 to 38) are expected over time (Rathi, Akshat and Huang, 2018[14]). Assuming that Chinese emission permits would trade at Yuan 250 per tonne of CO_2 (about EUR 32) and that the national ETS would cover 1.5 billion tonnes of CO_2 from the industrial sector, the carbon pricing gap at EUR 30 for the group of 42 countries would decline to 63%, from its current level of 76.5%. The carbon pricing gap for China itself would contract from 83% to 43%.

A recent reform of the EU ETS introduced a market stability reserve that will reduce the large surplus of emission permits in the trading system (European Union, 2018[15]). While price expectations for future permit prices are still moderate (see, e.g., ZEW (2018[16])), the EU directive allows to tighten the cap more strongly after 2024. A robust cap tightening could increase permit prices, as could the introduction of an auction reserve price, or a carbon floor price (as applicable in the United Kingdom (see Chapter 3).

> **Box 2.1. The carbon pricing gap**
>
> **The carbon pricing gap measures how much OECD and G20 economies together, as well as individually, fall short of pricing carbon emissions in line with a benchmark value.**
>
> The carbon pricing gap measures the difference between a benchmark value and the actual effective carbon rate (ECR) for every percentile of emissions, summing all positive differences. The report presents the carbon pricing gap as a percentage: If the ECR on all emissions was at least as high as the benchmark, the gap would be zero, and if the ECR was zero throughout, the gap would be 100%. Throughout the report two benchmark values are applied, EUR 30, a low-end estimate of the carbon costs today, and EUR 60, a midpoint estimate of the carbon costs in 2020 and a low-end estimate for 2030.
>
> The report presents the carbon pricing gap across the aggregate of all 42 OECD and G20 economies as well as at the level of individual countries. Within these groups, it can be considered across all economic sectors, or at the level of individual sectors.
>
> The aggregate carbon pricing gap indicates how advanced the 42 countries are with the implementation of market-based, cost-effective tools to decarbonise their economies. The measure describes the state of carbon pricing, and can be tracked across time and compared across companies and sectors. It can also be seen as indicative of countries' effort, through cost-effective policies, to reduce CO_2 emissions from energy use.
>
> At the country level, the gap also can be seen as an indicator of long-run competitiveness. A zero or very low gap signals to investors that a country seeks to decarbonise at lowest cost and that its companies are being incentivised to compete and thrive in a low-carbon economy. A high gap indicates either of two undesirable states of the economy. One, overly costly effort. The carbon pricing gap only considers market-based policies, alternative policies very likely reduce fewer emissions for each Euro invested in abatement. Two, limited overall effort. Firms are then more likely to forego the opportunities that arise in a low-carbon economy and face higher transition risks.
>
> Countries that pursue overly costly mitigation effort or no effort at all may also increase sovereign risk. A collapse in demand for fossil fuel, be it technology, consumer, litigation or policy driven could spark a global financial crisis (Mercure et al., 2018[17]). Carbon prices ensure that all economic actors account for carbon costs in their business decisions, making it costly to sustain the behavioural bias of ignoring the low-carbon transition. Increasing carbon prices gradually allows for a smooth reduction in the demand for fossil fuel, lowering the risk of an economic crisis caused by a collapse in demand for fossil fuel and the resulting devaluation of carbon intensive assets.

An increase in permit prices to at least EUR 30 would diminish the carbon pricing gap at EUR 30 from 52% today to 25% for the 22 EU countries participating in this study. The overall gap would decline by three percentage points. This may sound modest, but reflects the relatively higher starting point in the European Union as well as its share in aggregate emissions. Nevertheless, such a reform would contribute positively to overall carbon pricing momentum. Countries or regions can signal to investors that their climate policies are prudent yet ambitious, and that adaptation to a low-carbon economy goes hand in hand with strong economic performance.

Canada has increased carbon prices significantly in recent years. Design features, including the choice between taxes and trading systems, vary across provinces, but the federal carbon pricing backstop guarantees a common minimum of ambition across the country (Environment and Climate Change Canada, 2018[18]). As a result, the Canadian carbon pricing gap is expected to drop from 65% in 2015 to about 43% in 2018.[7] If all emissions are covered and the minimum carbon price increases as planned to CAD 50 (about EUR 32.5) per tonne of CO_2 by 2022, the carbon pricing gap at EUR 30 would reduce significantly.

The above-mentioned policies strongly reduce the carbon pricing gap within countries, meaning that they make substantially faster progress than others in reducing emissions through cost-effective action. There is substantial heterogeneity across countries. The aggregate carbon pricing gap at EUR 30 for the ten best performing countries is 44%. The ten countries that lag most behind have an aggregate gap of 85%.

The carbon pricing gap across sectors

The carbon pricing gap varies substantially across sectors. The gap at EUR 30 is lowest for road transport, at 21%, and highest for industry, at 91%. The gap is above 80% in the electricity and the residential and commercial sectors. In the electricity sector, 66% of emissions are now priced (see Figure 2.4). Closing the gap in the electricity sector is as much about pricing the remaining third of emissions as it is about increasing the price of already priced emissions. If permit prices in the Chinese national ETS increased to Yuan 250 per tonne of CO_2 (Rathi, Akshat and Huang, 2018[14]), the gap would decrease to 56%. In the industry sector and the residential and commercial sector, more than two thirds of emissions are still unpriced (Figure 2.4). Implementing carbon prices through taxes or emissions trading would be a first step towards closing the gap.

Table 2.3. Carbon pricing gap by sector

Carbon pricing gap in 42 OECD and G20 countries by sector

Sector	Carbon Pricing Gap at EUR 30	Carbon Pricing Gap at EUR 60
Agriculture & fisheries	64%	78%
Electricity	84%	92%
Industry	91%	95%
Offroad transport	56%	75%
Residential and commercial	87%	93%
Road transport	21%	58%

At EUR 60, the carbon pricing gap is wide in all sectors. It is lowest in road transport at 58%, and 90% or more in the electricity, the industry and the residential and commercial sectors.

While the carbon pricing gaps are smallest for road transport this does not necessarily mean that the road sector is necessarily best positioned to transition smoothly to a low-carbon economy without supplementary policies. Countries with relatively high carbon prices in transport tend to have significantly lower transport-related emissions at the same level of economic development (Sterner, 2007[19]), but transport-related emissions tend nevertheless to be significant even in countries with relatively high carbon rates. This reveals that abatement costs for fully decarbonising the sector have been high, and suggests that action needs to be taken now if decarbonisation is to materialise.

The existing transport infrastructure has generally been developed for the needs of fossil fuel-based vehicles. Upgrading the infrastructure to the needs for zero-carbon transport services seems necessary to enable further abatement (e.g. by easing access to zero-carbon vehicles, charging and fuelling stations, expanding zero-carbon mass transit, and encouraging shifts to more carbon-efficient transport modes).

By comparison, a carbon price of EUR 30 in the electricity sector can enable a fuel switch from coal to natural gas, which is half as emissions intensive. Emissions can decline quickly as the carbon price floor in the United Kingdom has shown (see Chapter 3). Deeper decarbonisation in the electricity sector requires appropriate market designs in addition (IEA, 2016[20]).

Fuel switches in the industrial sector and in the residential and commercial sector can also cut emissions significantly (e.g. from coal to gas, from oil and gas to carbon-neutral fuels, or directly from coal to carbon-neutral fuels). The carbon prices needed to enable fuel switches depend on the existing fuel mix and infrastructure (e.g. age and type of boilers to generate heat, availability of carbon-neutral fuels, etc.) and may thus vary across countries.

As a side effect of fuel switches, carbon pricing revenues at current effective carbon rates could decline, if in the short to medium run they are likely to rise. As carbon rates are significantly higher for petrol and diesel than for electricity, a switch to electric vehicles could lead to a significant drop in revenues, if carbon rates do not increase in the electricity sector. Charging per kilometre travelled is also a possibility to prevent the transport tax base from eroding over time (Van Dender, 2018[21]). Similarly, charging per kilowatt hour for electricity and heat services allows sustaining revenues from energy use.

Notes

[1] EUR – USD parity is assumed.

[2] The emission base includes domestic aviation, but excludes international aviation.

[3] Note that a right-skewed distribution with 90 % of emissions unpriced and 10% of emissions priced at EUR 350 implies an average rate of EUR 35. Such a distribution is very different from a uniform distribution where 100% of emissions are price at EUR 35, which also implies an average rate of EUR 35. Policy implications are also very different. In the first case, 90% of emissions are clearly priced below their social cost, while in the second case all emissions are priced above the low-end estimate of social costs.

[4] In the presence of only the global warming externality cost-effective abatement would call for all emissions facing the same price. Accounting for other externalities on top of global warming (e.g. local air pollution; noise, etc.) all emissions should face at least a certain price for cost-effective abatement.

[5] Note that if carbon prices are equal across emitters, yet expected to increase over time, it can be beneficial for emitters to invest in long-lived low-carbon assets with abatement costs higher than

the current carbon price (cf. Vogt-Schilb et al. 2018). Investors in low-carbon assets will benefit from not having to pay much higher carbon prices in the future.

[6] More generally, the Minsky moment refers to a situation where apparent economic stability breeds economic instability. In stable economic times investors take on more and more debt as it is seemingly safe. The increase in debt levels, however, makes the economy more prone to financial crisis, see the Economist (2016[91]). By analogy, a Climate Minsky moment can be characterised as a situation where investors continue to invest in high-carbon assets as they currently receive good returns. The continuation of financing of high-carbon assets, however, increase the risk of economic crisis when low-carbon technology becomes competitive or the carbon budget becomes stricter.

[7] It is assumed that the federal carbon pricing backstop will be implemented as announced in January 2018.

References

Ceres (2017), *Power Forward 3.0: How the largest U.S. companies are capturing business value while addressing climate change*, CDP, Calvert Research and Management, Ceres and WWF, https://www.ceres.org/resources/reports/power-forward-3 (accessed on 26 February 2018). [6]

Environment and Climate Change Canada (2018), *Technical Paper on the carbon pricing backstop*, Environment and Climate Change Canada, Gatineau, QC, https://www.canada.ca/content/dam/eccc/documents/pdf/20170518-2-en.pdf (accessed on 26 February 2018). [18]

European Systemic Risk Board (2016), "Too late, too sudden: Transition to a low-carbon economy and systemic risk", *Reports of the Advisory Scientific Committee* 6, https://www.esrb.europa.eu/pub/pdf/asc/Reports_ASC_6_1602.pdf (accessed on 20 February 2018). [4]

European Union (2018), *Directive of the European Parliament and the Council amending Directive 2003/87/EC to enhance cost-effective emission reductions and low-carbon investments and Decision (EU) 2015/1814*, http://data.consilium.europa.eu/doc/document/PE-63-2017-INIT/en/pdf (accessed on 27 February 2018). [15]

High-Level Commission on Carbon Prices (2017), *Report of the High-Level Commission on Carbon Prices*, World Bank, Washington, D.C., https://static1.squarespace.com/static/54ff9c5ce4b0a53decccfb4c/t/59b7f2409f8dce5316811916/1505227332748/CarbonPricing_FullReport.pdf (accessed on 16 February 2018). [3]

Hunt, C., O. Weber and T. Dordi (2017), "A comparative analysis of the anti-Apartheid and fossil fuel divestment campaigns", *Journal of Sustainable Finance & Investment*, Vol. 7/1, pp. 64-81, http://dx.doi.org/10.1080/20430795.2016.1202641. [8]

IEA (2016), *Re-powering Markets: Market design and regulation during the transition to low-carbon power systems*, IEA, Paris, https://www.iea.org/publications/freepublications/publication/REPOWERINGMARKETS.PDF (accessed on 21 February 2018). [20]

Kersting, S. and K. Stratmann (2018), "German businesses outpace politicians on carbon issues", *Handelsblatt*, https://global.handelsblatt.com/companies/german-businesses-outpace-politicians-carbon-issues-co2-climate-change-global-warming-888790 (accessed on 26 February 2018). [7]

Mercure, J. et al. (2018), "Macroeconomic impact of stranded fossil fuel assets", *Nature Climate Change*, Vol. 8, pp. 588-593, http://dx.doi.org/10.1038/s41558-018-0182-1. [17]

Nachmany, M. et al. (2017), *Global trends in climate change legislation and litigation*, Grantham Research Institute on Climate Change and the Enviornment, London, http://www.cccep.ac.uk (accessed on 23 February 2018). [10]

NDRC (2017), *National carbon emissions trading market construction program*, http://qhs.ndrc.gov.cn/zcfg/201712/W020171220577324953088.pdf. [13]

OECD (2018), *Taxing Energy Use 2018: Companion to the Taxing Energy Use Database*, OECD Publishing, Paris. [1]

OECD (2017), *Tax Policy Reforms 2017: OECD and Selected Partner Economies*, OECD Publishing, Paris, http://dx.doi.org/10.1787/9789264279919-en. [2]

Rathi, Akshat and Huang, E. (2018), *The complete guide to the world's largest carbon market that just launched in China*. [14]

Shankleman, J. and F. Lacqua (2017), *Carney's CEO Club Gives $3.3 Trillion Muscle to Climate Fight - Bloomberg*, Bloomberg, https://www.bloomberg.com/news/articles/2017-06-29/carney-s-ceo-club-gives-3-3-trillion-muscle-to-climate-fight (accessed on 26 February 2018). [12]

Sterner, T. (2007), "Fuel taxes: An important instrument for climate policy", *Energy Policy*, Vol. 35/6, pp. 3194-3202, http://dx.doi.org/10.1016/J.ENPOL.2006.10.025. [19]

TCFD (2017), *Recommendations of the Task Force on Climate-related Financial Disclosures: Final Report*, Financial Stability Board, Bank for International Settlements, https://www.fsb-tcfd.org/wp-content/uploads/2017/06/FINAL-TCFD-Report-062817.pdf (accessed on 23 February 2018). [5]

The Economist (2016), "Minsky's moment - Financial stability", *The Economist*, https://www.economist.com/news/economics-brief/21702740-second-article-our-series-seminal-economic-ideas-looks-hyman-minskys (accessed on 26 February 2018). [22]

UNEP (2017), *The Status of Climate Change Litigation. A global review.*, UN Environment Programme, Nairobi, http://columbiaclimatelaw.com/files/2017/05/Burger-Gundlach-2017-05-UN-Envt-CC-Litigation.pdf (accessed on 23 February 2018). [9]

Van Dender, K. (2018), "Taxing vehicles, fuel, and road use: what mix for road transport?", *forthcoming in: OECD Taxation Working Papers*, OECD Publishing, Paris. [21]

Zenghelis, D. and N. Stern (2016), "The importance of looking forward to manage risks: submission to the Task Force on Climate-Related Financial Disclosures", ESRC Centre for Climate Change Economics and Policy, London, http://www.cccep.ac.uk (accessed on 23 February 2018). [11]

ZEW (2018), *Energy Market Barometer: January-February 2018*, ZEW, Mannheim. [16]

Chapter 3. Carbon pricing in 2015 – Detailed analysis

This chapter provides an overview of the state of carbon pricing in 2015. It shows effective carbon rates for all 42 countries combined and separately by country, discusses change between 2012 and 2015, and puts carbon pricing in a broader economic context.

This chapter provides an overview of the state of carbon pricing in 2015. It shows effective carbon rates for all 42 countries combined and separately by country. A comparison at the level of sectors reveals that effective carbon rates do not only vary substantially across sectors (as discussed in the previous chapter), but also across countries within sectors. Comparing carbon rates in 2015 with those in 2012 shows that, while carbon rates tend to increase slowly on average, some countries have made significant progress with pricing emissions more in line with social costs and long-term emission reduction commitments.

Effective carbon rates in 2015 consist of tax rates as of 1 April 2015 (OECD, 2018[1]) and average permit prices from emission trading systems for 2015 (see Annex A for details on emissions trading systems). Emission data is for 2015 and calculated from fuel use as provided by the Extended World Energy Balances (EWEB) of the International Energy Agency (IEA, 2017[2]). The coverage of emissions trading systems is estimated based on data by the authorities governing the respective systems. Effective carbon rates for 2012 consist of tax rates as of 1 April 2012, average permit prices and ETS coverage for 2012, and emissions levels in 2012.[1]

Share of emissions priced and price levels across countries in 2015

Across all 42 OECD and G20 countries covered in this report, 44% of carbon emissions from energy use were subject to an effective carbon rate in 2015. Rate levels remained low, with only 12% of emissions priced above EUR 30, a conservative low-end estimate of the social costs of carbon emissions in 2015. Only 9% of emissions were priced at EUR 60 or more, a midpoint estimate of the carbon prices needed in 2020 for countries to be in line with reaching their commitments from the Paris Agreement, according to the High Level Commission on Carbon Prices (2017[3]).

Figure 3.1. Proportion of CO$_2$ emissions priced at different price levels in 2015

Price levels in EUR per tonne of CO$_2$

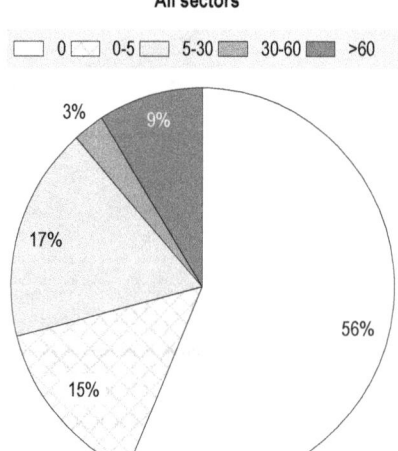

Aggregate numbers on carbon pricing can hide substantial differences across countries. While on aggregate 56% of emissions were unpriced across the 42 OECD and G20

countries, the simple (unweighted) average of unpriced emissions for the 42 countries was substantially lower, at 33%. This means that large emitters tend to price fewer emissions than countries that emit a smaller amount of emissions. In addition, large emitters also tend to set lower rates for those emissions that are subject to a price. While on aggregate 12% of emissions were priced above EUR 30 per tonne CO_2, the simple average of emissions priced above EUR 30 across the 42 countries was 27%.

Table 3.1 shows that 15 countries priced more than 80% of carbon emissions and five (Ireland, Israel, Korea, Luxembourg and the Netherlands) priced more than 90% of carbon emissions in 2015. Price levels were generally low, with only four countries (Luxembourg, Norway, Switzerland and the United Kingdom) pricing nearly half or more of their emissions above the low-end estimate of climate costs of EUR 30 per tonne of CO_2. Generally, few emissions were subject to an effective carbon rate above EUR 60 in 2015, and most of these emissions were from road transport. Table 3.6 provides more detail on effective carbon rates in the road sector.

Between 2012 and 2015, Korea and Mexico progressed strongly in pricing emissions. Korea introduced an emissions trading system, which covered most sectors of the economy in 2015, increasing the share of priced emissions by 51 percentage points, and the share of emissions priced above EUR 5 by 65 points. Mexico introduced a carbon tax in 2014 as well as increased effective excise tax rates on transport fuels (Arlinghaus and Van Dender, 2017[4]). The share of emissions priced increased by 26 percentage points (mainly through the carbon tax) and the share of emissions priced above EUR 60 per tonne of CO_2 rose by 30 percentage points (through higher effective excise taxes on transport fuels). Quebec in Canada and California in the United States introduced emissions trading systems in 2013, so increasing the share of priced emissions.

The large decrease in priced emissions in South Africa results from a zero rate for the slate levy, a tax on coal products, in 2015 (South African Treasury, 2015[5]). The decrease in effective carbon rate coverage above EUR 5 in Turkey results from a depreciation of the Turkish Lira against the Euro in the same time period.

As explained above, aggregate numbers can hide the substantial progress made by some countries, because large emitters tend to price fewer emissions than countries that emit a smaller amount of emissions. Nevertheless, the share of priced emissions increased by more than 5 percentage points between 2012 and 2015 for the 42 countries as a group. The share of emissions with an effective carbon rate above EUR 30 increased by two percentage points and the share above EUR 60 by nearly four percentage points.

Table 3.1. Proportion of emissions priced per tonne of CO$_2$ by country

Country	Proportion of emissions priced at or above in 2015 (in percent)				Change, from 2012 to 2015, of emissions priced at or above (in percentage points)			
	EUR 0	EUR 5	EUR 30	EUR 60	EUR 0	EUR 5	EUR 30	EUR 60
ARG	73%	24%	24%	20%	na	na	na	na
AUS	23%	23%	20%	20%	-1	-1	1	2
AUT	64%	64%	34%	25%	0	0	-7	1
BEL	72%	64%	23%	23%	-7	-2	1	1
BRA	33%	25%	0%	0%	-1	-2	0	0
CAN	61%	61%	16%	0%	na	na	na	na
CHE	87%	78%	70%	36%	1	-4	0	1
CHL	20%	20%	20%	9%	4	4	4	2
CHN	22%	9%	9%	9%	11	1	1	9
CZE	79%	67%	15%	15%	7	2	1	1
DEU	88%	87%	19%	19%	5	4	0	1
DNK	78%	78%	32%	31%	5	5	-20	-1
ESP	86%	84%	34%	28%	15	14	5	5
EST	76%	71%	13%	11%	-4	3	0	0
FIN	62%	62%	42%	26%	-2	-2	1	1
FRA	83%	82%	42%	35%	7	8	9	2
GBR	76%	75%	49%	27%	-4	-4	20	3
GRC	90%	90%	31%	25%	-1	-2	2	4
HUN	64%	61%	22%	22%	2	0	4	4
IDN	16%	16%	0%	0%	0	0	0	0
IND	64%	18%	9%	2%	3	7	7	0
IRL	93%	93%	36%	29%	4	4	0	-1
ISL	78%	78%	38%	38%	0	0	-4	-4
ISR	98%	29%	27%	27%	1	-5	-5	-5
ITA	88%	87%	40%	37%	0	2	-2	1
JPN	85%	40%	21%	18%	-2	19	3	1
KOR	97%	97%	16%	16%	51	65	2	3
LUX	96%	85%	64%	64%	2	-1	2	2
LVA	55%	46%	24%	22%	na	na	na	na
MEX	62%	32%	30%	30%	26	2	30	30
NLD	94%	94%	38%	33%	8	9	2	-2
NOR	82%	81%	61%	56%	1	1	0	19
NZL	76%	20%	20%	19%	9	1	1	1
POL	83%	74%	15%	15%	9	4	1	1
PRT	78%	76%	28%	25%	5	6	0	-1
RUS	35%	0%	0%	0%	-6	0	0	0
SVK	79%	69%	26%	16%	-1	-1	-4	0
SVN	82%	82%	46%	42%	-1	1	7	9
SWE	58%	58%	25%	25%	5	6	1	3
TUR	49%	23%	21%	20%	2	-20	3	5
USA	37%	37%	3%	0%	5	9	3	0
ZAF	12%	11%	11%	10%	-46	-1	0	-1

Note: na: not available. The left side of the table shows the proportion of emissions with an ECR above EUR 0, 5, 30 and 60 in per cent. The right hand side shows the change in the proportion of emissions with an ECR above EUR 0, 5, 30 and 60 from 2012 to 2015, in percentage points. The table includes emissions from the combustion of biomass in the emission base. Annex 3.A shows results excluding emissions from the combustion of biomass in the emission base.

Priced emissions in the electricity sector in 2015

While in 2015 two-thirds of aggregate emissions from the electricity sector in the 42 countries as a group were not priced, the simple average of the share of priced emissions across the 42 countries was 62%. This means that countries with high emissions from the electricity sector tended to price fewer emissions than countries with a smaller amount of emissions. Only 1% of aggregate emissions were priced above of EUR 30 per tonne of CO_2, while the simple average across the 42 countries was 3%.

Thirteen countries priced close to 100% of emissions from the electricity sector, see Table 3.3. The effective carbon rates in the electricity sector arose mostly from emissions trading systems, but Argentina, India and Israel priced large shares of electricity emissions through taxes. Most countries with nationwide emissions trading systems covered nearly all of their electricity emissions. Coverage below 100% can occur through electricity generated from biomass, for which the rate is generally zero, and small power plants, often CHP plants, below the threshold for inclusion in the system.

Emission permits traded at values between about EUR 5 to 15 in 2015. Combined with the fact that emissions trading was the main carbon pricing instrument in the electricity sector, this means that the share of emissions priced above EUR 5 was similar to the share of priced emissions for many countries. Only a few countries priced a significant share of electricity emissions at EUR 30 and above in 2015. In the United Kingdom, 79% of electricity emissions where priced above EUR 30 per tonne CO_2 in 2015.

The United Kingdom introduced a Carbon Price Support (CPS) in 2013 at GBP 9 per tonne of CO_2 for emissions in the electricity sector. The carbon price support is charged on top of permit prices and increased to GBP 18 by 1 April 2015. The total effective carbon rate has been slightly over EUR 30 per tonne CO_2 since then.

Table 3.2. Emissions from electricity generation fall sharply with the introduction of a carbon price support

Carbon dioxide emissions in the United Kingdom before and after the introduction of the carbon price support

		2012	2016	Change (2012-2016)	Change in %
Electricity sector	CO_2 emissions in Mt	158	66	-92	-58%
	Coal use in Mt	54	12	42	-78%
	Carbon Price Support (CPS) per tonne of CO_2	0	GBP 18 (EUR 24.80)	GBP 18 (EUR 24.80)	
	Permit Price in EU ETS in EUR per tonne of CO_2	7.24	7.6	0.36	+5%
	Effective Carbon Rate in EUR per tonne of CO_2	7.24	32.40	25.16	+347%
Entire economy	CO_2 emissions in Mt	474	356	-118	-25%
	Reductions from electricity sector			-92	-19%

Sources: Hirst (2018[6]), European Energy Exchange (2015[7]), UK Department for Business, Energy & Industrial Strategy (2017[8]), UK Department for Business, Energy & Industrial Strategy (2018[9])

Emissions from the electricity sector decreased by 58% from 2012, before the CPS was introduced, *to 2016, the first full year for which total effective carbon rates equalled about EUR 30* (see Table 3.2). The decrease in emissions is explained by a sharp drop in the use of coal for the generation of electricity. Coal use fell by 78% in the same period.

Coal was partly replaced natural gas, which is about half as emission intensive as coal per unit of energy, and partly by zero-carbon renewables.

Overall UK emissions from energy use fell by 25% in between 2012 and 2016, of which 19 percentage points can be attributed to cleaner electricity generation. British greenhouse gas emission are now below the level of 1890 (Hausfather (2018[10]), Ward (2018[11])). The British experience show how fast emissions can decline if carbon prices are at levels high enough to encourage a switch to cleaner fuels. The Dutch coalition treaty of 2017 follows on the British example by including the introduction of a minimum price for emissions covered by the EU ETS.

California included a minimum auction price for its permits when it started its cap and trade program in 2013. The minimum price increases by 5% plus inflation each year. While prices were still fairly moderate in 2015 at about USD 13 per tonne of CO_2, the mandated increase in the auction price ensures that carbon price levels reach at least about EUR 30 in 2030. Ontario and Quebec follow the same approach.

The EU will introduce a Market Stability Reserve (MSR) for its ETS in 2019 (European Union, 2018[12]). The market stability reserve will remove 24% of surplus permits from the market, if the surplus of permits exceeds 833 million. A surplus of permit occurs when aggregate verified emissions are below the emission cap. The MSR will release permits into the market if the surplus falls below 400 million permits. From 2023 onwards, allowances held in the reserve that exceed the total number of allowances auctioned during the previous year they will become invalid. Research by Enerdata (2018[13]) suggests that even with the MSR, permit prices will hardly increase up to mid-2030s.[2] The authors expect that the cap becomes binding only in the 2030s. Once the surplus of permits disappears, prices may soon increase. A fast increase in carbon emission prices, projected from the mid- or end-2030s onwards, can trigger a sudden loss of value of carbon intensive assets; especially if the price rise is unexpected (see the section discussing the *carbon pricing gap*). A minimum auction price that increases by a fixed percentage plus inflation would allow a smooth increase of carbon pricing and prevent sudden asset price revaluations.

Korea and Mexico significantly expanded their carbon pricing base in the electricity sector from 2012 to 2015. The new Korean ETS increased the share of priced electricity emissions by 77 percentage points. Mexico's carbon tax increased the share of priced electricity emissions by 45 percentage points. China's ETS pilots increased the share of priced emissions in the electricity sector to 14%.

As already mentioned in the previous subsection, the large decrease in priced emissions in South Africa results from a zero rate for the slate levy in 2015 (South African Treasury, 2015[5]). The significant decrease in the share of electricity emissions priced above EUR 5 in Turkey results from a depreciation of the Turkish Lira against the Euro. Israel used less oil products in 2015 compared to 2012, which are taxed at relatively high effective carbon rates, to generate electricity.

Table 3.3. Proportion of emissions priced in the electricity sector per tonne of CO_2 by country

Country	Proportion of emissions priced at or above in 2015 (in percent)				Change, from 2012 to 2015, of emissions priced at or above (in percentage points)			
	EUR 0	EUR 5	EUR 30	EUR 60	EUR 0	EUR 5	EUR 30	EUR 60
ARG	74%	13%	13%	0%	na	na	na	na
AUS	0%	0%	0%	0%	0	0	0	0
AUT	66%	66%	0%	0%	-5	-5	0	0
BEL	70%	69%	0%	0%	2	1	0	0
BRA	10%	10%	0%	0%	-10	-10	0	0
CAN	54%	54%	0%	0%	na	na	na	na
CHE	29%	29%	29%	0%	6	6	29	0
CHL	0%	0%	0%	0%	0	0	0	0
CHN	14%	0%	0%	0%	14	0	0	0
CZE	96%	96%	0%	0%	0	0	0	0
DEU	90%	90%	0%	0%	-1	-1	0	0
DNK	73%	73%	0%	0%	-5	-5	0	0
ESP	95%	95%	0%	0%	-2	-2	0	0
EST	88%	88%	0%	0%	2	2	0	0
FIN	70%	70%	0%	0%	4	4	0	0
FRA	91%	91%	0%	0%	-6	-6	0	0
GBR	87%	87%	79%	0%	-10	-10	79	0
GRC	99%	99%	12%	2%	0	0	-2	0
HUN	77%	77%	0%	0%	-8	-8	0	0
IDN	0%	0%	0%	0%	0	0	0	0
IND	98%	0%	0%	0%	2	0	0	0
IRL	97%	97%	0%	0%	0	0	0	0
ISL	0%	0%	0%	0%	0	0	0	0
ISR	100%	1%	1%	1%	0	-13	-13	-13
ITA	88%	88%	0%	0%	-2	1	0	0
JPN	89%	13%	0%	0%	-2	11	-2	-2
KOR	100%	100%	0%	0%	77	81	0	0
LUX	64%	64%	0%	0%	-27	-27	0	0
LVA	64%	64%	0%	0%	na	na	na	na
MEX	47%	1%	1%	1%	45	0	1	1
NLD	97%	97%	0%	0%	5	5	0	0
NOR	66%	66%	0%	0%	-2	-2	0	0
NZL	82%	0%	0%	0%	12	0	0	0
POL	94%	94%	0%	0%	0	0	0	0
PRT	93%	93%	0%	0%	0	0	0	0
RUS	0%	0%	0%	0%	-4	0	0	0
SVK	85%	85%	0%	0%	-5	-5	0	0
SVN	98%	98%	0%	0%	0	0	0	0
SWE	30%	30%	0%	0%	6	6	0	0
TUR	32%	0%	0%	0%	-4	-36	0	0
USA	8%	8%	0%	0%	4	8	0	0
ZAF	0%	0%	0%	0%	-100	0	0	0

Note: na: not available. The left side of the table shows the proportion of emissions with an ECR above EUR 0, 5, 30 and 60 in percent. The right-hand side shows the change in the proportion of emissions with an ECR above EUR 0, 5, 30 and 60 from 2012 to 2015, in percentage points. The table includes emissions from the combustion of biomass in the emission base. Annex 3.A shows results excluding emissions from the combustion of biomass in the emission base.

Priced emissions in the industry sector in 2015

In the industry sector, 65% of aggregate emissions from the 42 OECD and G20 countries covered in this report were unpriced in 2015. Only 2% of emissions faced an effective carbon rates larger than EUR 30 per tonne CO_2. In 2012, 72% of aggregate emissions had no price.

Countries with high emissions tended to price fewer industry emissions than countries with lower amounts of industry emissions. The (unweighted) average of priced emissions across the 42 countries was 60% for industry emissions. At the same time, over a quarter of all countries analysed priced 80% of industry emissions. Rates are often above EUR 5 but significantly below EUR 30 per tonne CO_2.

Few countries price a significant share of industrial emissions above EUR 30 per tonne of CO_2. In Norway, natural gas used in oil and gas extraction is covered by a carbon tax in addition to being covered by the EU ETS. In Finland and Slovenia, all firms pay carbon taxes for fossil-fuel use independently of whether they participate in the EU ETS or not (OECD, 2018, p. 20[1]). Slovenia expanded the carbon tax base to include all fossil fuels, whereas in 2012, the carbon tax applied only to natural gas.

The new Korean ETS increased the carbon price base in industry between 2012 and 2015 by 55 percentage points, to 98% (Table 3.4). The share of industry emissions priced above EUR 5 increased by 86 percentage points.

This report, including Table 3.4 shows the share of emissions priced above benchmark values of effective *marginal* carbon rates for the 42 countries. More than 35% of the effective marginal carbon rates in industry stem from emissions trading systems (see Table 2.2). Industrial facilities subject to an ETS often receive a significant share of emission permits for free. The effective *marginal* carbon rate does not account for the free allocation of permits; it only takes the marginal permit price into account.

Flues and Van Dender (2017[14]) discuss how free allocation of permits can lower the incentives of firms to invest in clean technologies. They calculate an effective *average* carbon rate that takes into account free permit allocation and provides information on the strength of the incentives to invest in clean technologies.

Table 3.4. **Proportion of emissions priced in the industry sector per tonne of CO_2 by country**

Country	Proportion of emissions priced at or above in 2015 (in percent)				Change, from 2012 to 2015, of emissions priced at or above (in percentage points)			
	EUR 0	EUR 5	EUR 30	EUR 60	EUR 0	EUR 5	EUR 30	EUR 60
ARG	62%	2%	2%	1%	na	na	na	na
AUS	3%	3%	3%	3%	-6	-6	3	3
AUT	54%	54%	11%	3%	1	1	-6	0
BEL	59%	57%	0%	0%	-14	-10	0	0
BRA	16%	2%	0%	0%	3	0	0	0
CAN	51%	51%	0%	0%	na	na	na	na
CHE	84%	49%	18%	0%	2	-15	-1	0
CHL	0%	0%	0%	0%	0	0	0	0
CHN	19%	2%	2%	1%	11	0	0	1
CZE	85%	50%	0%	0%	33	7	0	0
DEU	85%	82%	1%	0%	20	19	-2	0
DNK	86%	86%	13%	10%	16	16	-52	-3
ESP	74%	68%	4%	0%	14	9	1	0
EST	63%	45%	4%	0%	-20	6	0	0
FIN	60%	60%	42%	17%	-2	-2	1	4
FRA	79%	75%	2%	0%	1	4	-1	0
GBR	81%	79%	8%	4%	0	-2	-13	-3
GRC	91%	90%	16%	5%	-1	-2	-6	-2
HUN	79%	67%	3%	3%	0	-8	1	1
IDN	0%	0%	0%	0%	0	0	0	0
IND	71%	25%	1%	0%	2	21	0	0
IRL	72%	72%	3%	0%	-3	-1	-14	-8
ISL	24%	24%	0%	0%	3	3	0	0
ISR	85%	6%	0%	0%	7	4	-2	-2
ITA	97%	96%	2%	2%	4	10	-19	-5
JPN	70%	34%	5%	4%	-3	27	4	4
KOR	98%	97%	2%	2%	55	86	0	2
LUX	89%	77%	0%	0%	11	19	0	0
LVA	51%	29%	0%	0%	na	na	na	na
MEX	44%	4%	4%	4%	24	1	4	4
NLD	90%	89%	17%	2%	18	23	15	1
NOR	80%	79%	46%	46%	-7	-8	-9	28
NZL	54%	1%	1%	0%	10	0	0	0
POL	91%	65%	1%	1%	8	-4	0	0
PRT	65%	60%	3%	0%	11	8	1	0
RUS	44%	0%	0%	0%	-12	0	0	0
SVK	72%	56%	11%	0%	1	1	-5	0
SVN	86%	86%	39%	38%	1	13	32	32
SWE	54%	54%	4%	3%	8	8	1	3
TUR	41%	13%	4%	0%	-8	-23	-5	-1
USA	7%	7%	0%	0%	7	7	0	0
ZAF	4%	4%	4%	1%	-5	0	0	-3

Note: na: not available. The left side of the table shows the proportion of emissions with an ECR above EUR 0, 5, 30 and 60 in percent. The right hand side shows the change in the proportion of emissions with an ECR above EUR 0, 5, 30 and 60 from 2012 to 2015 in percentage points. The table includes emissions from the combustion of biomass in the emission base. Annex 3.A shows results excluding emissions from the combustion of biomass in the emission base.

Priced emissions in the residential and commercial sector in 2015

In the residential and commercial sector, 79% of aggregate emissions in the 42 OECD and G20 countries covered in this report were unpriced in 2015. Six percent of emissions faced a price above EUR 30 per tonne CO_2. In 2012, 81% of emissions from the residential and commercial sector were unpriced.

Like for other sectors, inter-country differences are large, and many countries price a significant share of emissions from the residential and commercial sector. The unweighted average of the share of priced emissions is 46% across the 42 countries, the unweighted cross-country share of prices above EUR 30 and EUR 60 per tonne CO_2 is 13% and 7% respectively.

Several countries price almost all residential and commercial emissions and some price these emissions at significant rates. Eight countries price more than 90% of emissions. The Netherlands and Switzerland price more than 80% of residential and commercial emissions above EUR 30 per tonne CO_2. The effective carbon rate in the residential and commercial sector generally consists of both excise and carbon taxes.

In France, the share of residential and commercial emissions priced above EUR 30 increased by 23 percentage points between 2012 and 2015. Energy taxes in France have a carbon component which increases over time (Ministère de la Transition écologique et solidaire de la République Francaise, 2018[15]). In 2017, the carbon component reached EUR 30.5 per tonne of CO_2, meaning that at the time of publication of this report, the vast majority of residential and commercial emissions will be priced above EUR 30 per tonne. By 2022, the carbon component is set to reach EUR 86 per tonne of CO_2.

In Japan, the share of emissions priced above EUR 30 in the residential and commercial sector increased strongly as tax rates rose. The Swiss carbon tax, which applies to fuels used in the residential and commercial sector, increased from CHF 36 (about EUR 30) to CHF 60 (about EUR 50) per tonne of CO_2 in 2014, because Switzerland had not reached its CO_2 emission reduction goal for 2012 (Le Conseil fédéral suisse, 2013[16]). In 2016, the carbon tax increased to CHF 84 (about EUR 70) per tonne of CO_2 (Le Conseil fédéral suisse, 2015[17]), so that now the majority or commercial and residential emissions are priced above EUR 60 (not shown in Table 3.5)

A number of countries expanded carbon rate coverage at rates below EUR 30 per tonne significantly between 2015 and 2012, mainly through taxing previously untaxed fuels. Iceland increased the share of priced emissions by 74 percentage points by expanding its carbon tax base to gaseous fuels. Mexico increased the share of priced emissions by 39 percentage points, mainly through the introduction of a carbon tax (OECD, 2018[1]). Spain expanded its taxbase to include biofuels for heating purposes and removed tax exemptions for natural gas and LPG. The share of priced emissions increased by 42 percentage points between 2012 and 2015. Ireland introduced a tax on solid fossil fuels in 2013, increasing the share of priced emissions in the residential and commercial sector by 23 percentage points. Poland introduced an excise duty on gaseous fuels in 2013. Its share of priced residential and commercial emissions increased by 23 percentage points.

Table 3.5. Proportion of emissions priced in the residential and commercial sector per tonne of CO_2 by country

Country	Proportion of emissions priced at or above in 2015 (in percent)				Change, from 2012 to 2015, of emissions priced at or above (in percentage points)			
	EUR 0	EUR 5	EUR 30	EUR 60	EUR 0	EUR 5	EUR 30	EUR 60
ARG	92%	1%	1%	0%	na	na	na	na
AUS	0%	0%	0%	0%	-15	-15	0	0
AUT	49%	49%	23%	0%	-3	-3	-26	0
BEL	73%	43%	0%	0%	-15	1	0	0
BRA	0%	0%	0%	0%	0	0	0	0
CAN	25%	25%	0%	0%	13	13	0	0
CHE	80%	80%	80%	0%	-1	-1	0	0
CHL	3%	3%	0%	0%	3	3	0	0
CHN	8%	6%	6%	5%	3	0	0	5
CZE	14%	13%	0%	0%	-21	-1	0	0
DEU	79%	78%	1%	1%	-3	-3	0	0
DNK	37%	37%	28%	28%	-8	-8	-16	-16
ESP	68%	68%	23%	0%	42	43	1	0
EST	18%	18%	5%	0%	1	2	-1	0
FIN	30%	30%	30%	29%	-2	-2	-1	0
FRA	66%	66%	23%	0%	21	24	23	0
GBR	27%	27%	4%	0%	-4	-4	-6	0
GRC	63%	62%	10%	9%	-3	-3	5	4
HUN	18%	18%	0%	0%	1	1	0	0
IDN	0%	0%	0%	0%	0	0	0	0
IND	4%	0%	0%	0%	0	0	0	0
IRL	97%	97%	23%	0%	23	23	2	0
ISL	100%	100%	0%	0%	74	74	0	0
ISR	97%	97%	0%	0%	34	34	0	0
ITA	68%	68%	52%	46%	-1	-1	-1	-1
JPN	100%	64%	31%	18%	0	48	30	17
KOR	86%	86%	16%	12%	-2	10	8	12
LUX	94%	47%	0%	0%	-1	-9	0	0
LVA	22%	20%	1%	1%	na	na	na	na
MEX	40%	1%	1%	1%	39	0	1	1
NLD	90%	90%	90%	90%	-1	-1	-1	-1
NOR	29%	29%	29%	25%	0	0	1	-1
NZL	63%	4%	4%	0%	38	0	0	0
POL	31%	24%	0%	0%	23	21	0	0
PRT	44%	44%	7%	5%	15	35	-1	-2
RUS	8%	0%	0%	0%	-1	0	0	0
SVK	93%	84%	28%	0%	3	2	-3	0
SVN	34%	34%	18%	0%	-3	-3	-6	0
SWE	20%	20%	20%	20%	-2	-2	-2	-2
TUR	45%	4%	4%	4%	13	-28	1	1
USA	5%	5%	0%	0%	5	5	0	0
ZAF	2%	0%	0%	0%	0	-1	0	0

Note: na: not available. The table includes emissions from the combustion of biomass in the emission base. Annex 3.A shows results excluding emissions from the combustion of biomass in the emission base.

Priced emissions in the road sector in 2015

Nearly all emissions (97%) of the road sector were priced in 2015. Effective carbon rates were significantly higher than in other sectors. 56% of aggregate emissions of the 42 countries covered have a rate above EUR 30 per tonne of CO_2, and 47% also exceed EUR 60 per tonne of CO_2. Compared to 2012, the share of emissions priced above EUR 60 increased by about 17 percentage points.

Many countries price close to or even 100% of road emissions above EUR 60 per tonne of CO_2. The unweighted average of the share of emissions priced above EUR 60 across the 42 countries is 81%. More than three quarter of all analysed countries price 90% of road emissions above EUR 30.

From 2012 to 2015, Mexico increased the share of emissions priced above EUR 60 by 98 percentage points through reforming its excise tax regime for road fuels (Arlinghaus and Van Dender, 2017[4]). India increased the share of emissions priced above EUR 30 by 73 percentage points in the same period by increasing tax rates on road fuels.

The shares of priced emissions are calculated on the basis of fuel sold in the respective countries, as recorded in the IEA's (2017[2]) extended world energy balances. This implies that countries that sell more fuel than used in their territory record higher emissions than if fuels used were the emission base. The energy balances do not record the amount of fuel used in a country. Countries with a high share of transit traffic and non-residents filling up their vehicles in its territories may thus record more emissions on the fuels sold compared to the fuel used base, especially when fuels are priced at a lower rate than in neighbouring countries. Other countries correspondingly show fewer emissions from sales than would be recorded on the basis of usage. OECD (2016, pp. 48-49[18]) provides more detail on countries' shares of emissions from road transport in their overall emissions.

Table 3.6. Proportion of emissions priced in the road sector per tonne of CO_2 by country

Country	Proportion of emissions priced at or above in 2015 (in percent)				Change, from 2012 to 2015, of emissions priced at or above (in percentage points)			
	EUR 0	EUR 5	EUR 30	EUR 60	EUR 0	EUR 5	EUR 30	EUR 60
ARG	92%	92%	92%	92%	na	na	na	na
AUS	99%	99%	99%	95%	-1	-1	3	0
AUT	92%	92%	92%	92%	-2	-2	-2	-2
BEL	96%	96%	96%	96%	1	1	1	1
BRA	74%	74%	0%	0%	-7	-7	0	0
CAN	100%	100%	67%	0%	na	na	na	na
CHE	99%	99%	99%	99%	-1	-1	-1	-1
CHL	100%	100%	100%	43%	0	0	0	3
CHN	93%	93%	93%	93%	-1	-1	-1	93
CZE	95%	95%	95%	93%	0	0	0	0
DEU	99%	99%	99%	99%	-1	-1	-1	-1
DNK	94%	94%	94%	94%	0	0	0	0
ESP	100%	100%	99%	99%	8	8	7	7
EST	99%	99%	99%	99%	0	0	0	0
FIN	87%	87%	87%	87%	-13	-13	-13	-12
FRA	100%	100%	100%	100%	0	0	0	0
GBR	100%	100%	100%	100%	0	0	0	0
GRC	100%	100%	100%	100%	0	0	0	0
HUN	100%	100%	100%	100%	4	4	4	5
IDN	97%	97%	0%	0%	-1	-1	0	0
IND	97%	97%	97%	29%	0	0	73	5
IRL	100%	100%	100%	100%	0	0	0	0
ISL	95%	95%	95%	95%	-5	-5	-5	-5
ISR	100%	100%	100%	100%	0	0	0	0
ITA	100%	98%	98%	98%	0	0	0	0
JPN	100%	100%	100%	98%	0	0	0	0
KOR	99%	99%	96%	96%	0	0	0	0
LUX	100%	100%	100%	100%	2	2	2	2
LVA	99%	99%	99%	93%	na	na	na	na
MEX	100%	98%	98%	98%	1	-1	98	98
NLD	100%	100%	100%	100%	0	0	0	3
NOR	100%	100%	100%	100%	0	0	0	0
NZL	100%	55%	55%	54%	0	-2	-2	-2
POL	99%	99%	99%	99%	4	4	4	4
PRT	94%	94%	94%	94%	-1	-1	-1	0
RUS	99%	0%	0%	0%	0	0	0	0
SVK	93%	93%	93%	93%	-3	-3	-3	-3
SVN	98%	98%	98%	98%	1	1	1	1
SWE	85%	85%	85%	85%	-7	-6	-6	-6
TUR	100%	100%	100%	100%	0	0	0	0
USA	100%	100%	9%	0%	0	0	9	0
ZAF	100%	100%	100%	100%	0	0	0	0

Note: na: not available. The table includes emissions from the combustion of biomass in the emission base. Annex 3.A shows results excluding emissions from the combustion of biomass in the emission base.

Box 3.1. External costs in road transport

Many countries price all of their emission from road transport above EUR 60 per tonne CO_2. Does this mean that effective carbon rates in the road sector are high enough? Not necessarily.

Road use gives rise to a range of external costs including congestion, noise, accidents and local air pollution in addition to the damage caused by CO_2 emissions. Taxes on transport fuels, which account for 99% of the effective carbon rate in road transport, are a second-best instrument to internalise road use related externalities. This implies that ideally the prevailing taxes on transport energy should be compared to the full range of external costs that they are intended to cover.

A comparison of all road use related external costs is beyond the scope of the report, but an effective carbon rate of more than EUR 30 now, and EUR 60 forward looking, is justifiable. The first reason is that EUR 30 per tonne of CO_2 is a low-end estimate today's climate costs from carbon alone, EUR 60 is a low-end estimate of the climate costs in 2030 (High-Level Commission on Carbon Prices, 2017[3]) and true climate costs can be substantially higher than the low-end estimates. The second reason is that other external costs matter, and these can be high. While detailed information on the level of these costs is not at hand for all countries, some rough indications is extracted from Van Dender (2018[19]), which itself builds on sources from the European Union, France and the United Kingdom.

Based on back-of-the-envelope calculations, Figure 3.2 shows the sum of marginal external costs associated with a litre of fuel use, for France and the United Kingdom, averaged across gasoline and diesel and distinguishing between urban and rural driving. As can be seen, in the two leftmost columns, the external costs are much larger for urban driving. This is mainly because of higher congestion costs, and to a lesser extent because of greater exposure to air pollution.

In order to compare excise taxes with external costs, to know if they are approximately aligned, the external costs of congestion need downward adjustment to account for the fact that car users respond to higher fuel taxes partly by driving less (which reduces congestion) but also by investing more in fuel economy (which does not reduce congestion). Since evidence indicates that both responses are about equally large in the long run, the adjustment factor for congestion costs is 50%, as an order of magnitude. The scaled down external costs estimates are shown in the middle two columns of Figure 3.2, label mec-ft (for marginal external costs relevant to fuel tax comparison).

The adjusted marginal external costs are compared to the prevailing excise taxes. Keeping in mind that both sets of numbers (taxes and marginal external costs) are estimates, the insight is that fuel taxes appear adequately aligned with the marginal external costs of rural driving, and well below those of urban driving.

Figure 3.2. Estimates of marginal external costs and of fuel tax, France and United Kingdom, in EUR per litre of gasoline and diesel

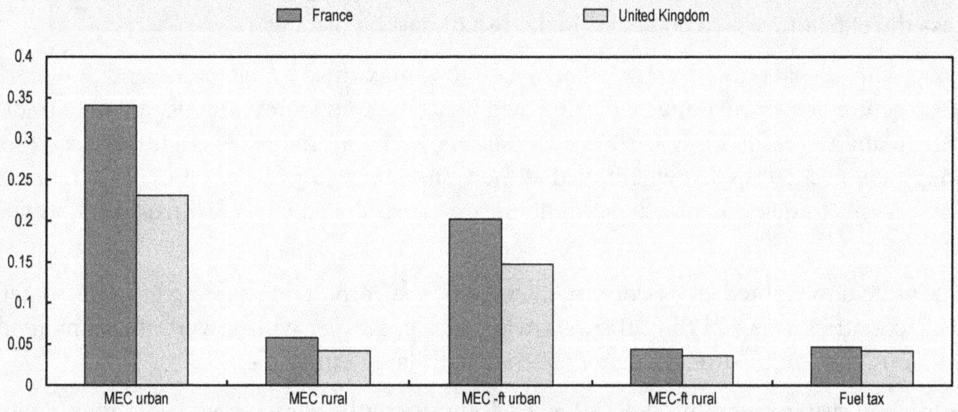

Note: MEC = marginal external cost; urban = driving in urban environments; MEC-ft = MEC as relevant to the fuel tax, i.e.. after correction for indirect impact of fuel costs on driving-related external costs; rural = driving in rural environments (to be understood as non-urban).
Source: (OECD, 2018[1])

Are fuel taxes then on average too low? The main difference between urban and rural driving pertains to congestion costs. Since congestion costs in rural driving are very low, the answer to this question depends on one's view on how to address congestion best. As explained in more detail in Van Dender (2018[19]), fuel taxes are not very well suited for curbing congestion, and electronic charging mechanisms allow for better internalisation of congestion costs. If, however, the view is that more sophisticated congestion pricing or other congestion management policies remain elusive, then higher fuel taxes appear to be justified based on the estimates presented in Figure 3.2.

However, to allow for better congestion management and anticipating on eventual decarbonisation of road transport, it may be better to argue for more sophisticated congestion pricing than for increasing fuel taxes to reflect average congestion. Fuel taxes then would be 'about right' based on Figure 3.2. At this point, however, it is worth noting that the marginal external cost estimates used for Figure 3.2 should be considered as low-end estimates, particularly for air pollution, where they assume compliance with emission standards.

In sum, since fuel taxes appear to align with low end estimates of marginal external costs, and since they are in the vicinity of marginal external costs only where congestion costs are very low, current fuel taxes in France and the United Kingdom are at the low end of appropriate levels. Moderate increases are likely to engender further social benefits. If fuel taxes are thought to have a role in curbing congestion, then they at present appear to be too low. These results are similar to those of a more comprehensive exercise for EU countries (Santos, 2017[20]).

Sources: Adapted from OECD (2018[1]), OECD (2016[18]) and Van Dender (2018[19])

Carbon pricing gap across countries in 2015

The carbon pricing gap at EUR 30 was 79.5% for the 42 countries as a group in 2015. As described in Box 2.1 in more detail, the carbon pricing gap is a summary indicator to assess the extent to which countries make use of carbon pricing.

A zero gap signals to investors that a country maximises abatement and low-carbon infrastructure for each dollar invested and that its companies are on a good track to compete and thrive in a low-carbon economy. A high gap indicates countries spend more money than needed on abatement or that their climate policy is not on track to meet their commitments to decarbonise their economies as agreed at the UN Climate Conference in Paris.

The simple unweighted cross-country average of the carbon pricing gap at EUR 30 across the 42 countries was 62% in 2015, showing that countries with fewer emissions tend to price emissions more strongly than countries with large emissions.

The carbon pricing gap at EUR 30 varied significantly across countries, ranging from 27% to 100%. This shows that some countries had significantly advanced in pricing emissions, while others had hardly started doing so.

Carbon pricing progressed compared to 2012, also in countries with high emissions. The aggregate gap declined by 3 percentage points compared to 2012, the unweighted cross-country average by 2 percentage points.

Korea, Mexico and the United Kingdom substantially reduced their carbon pricing gaps between 2012 and 2015, see Table 3.7. Korea's carbon pricing gap shrank by 30 percentage points to 43% in 2015, mainly through the introduction of its emission trading system. Mexico reformed its excise duties on transport fuels and introduced a carbon tax, reducing its carbon pricing gap by 23 percentage points. The United Kingdom lowered its gap to 42% in 2015 from 56% in 2012 by introducing a price floor for carbon emission from the electricity sector.

France decreased its carbon pricing gap by nine percentage points each between 2015 and 2012, increasing the carbon component rates in its excise duties on fuels. The Chinese gap declined slightly, mainly through its regional pilot emission trading systems. A substantially bigger drop in the Chinese gap is expected through the introduction of its national ETS, see the section on *How countries can reduce the carbon pricing gap* on page 31 in Chapter 2.

Note that the carbon pricing gap can also change unintentionally over time for several reasons. First, where substitute fuels subject to different rates exist, fuel substitution can affect the carbon pricing gap. For example, dieselisation of road transport tends to increase the carbon pricing gap, given the relatively low taxes on diesel. Second, by leaving tax rates unchanged in nominal terms and not adjusting them for inflation, tax rates will decrease in real terms over time. Over time, this increases the carbon pricing gap.

Table 3.7. Carbon pricing gap at EUR 30 in 2015

Country	2015	2012
ARG	76%	na
AUS	79%	78%
AUT	51%	52%
BEL	65%	65%
BRA	94%	88%
CAN	65%	na
CHE	27%	20%
CHL	80%	84%
CHN	90%	92%
CZE	70%	71%
DEU	53%	53%
DNK	52%	40%
ESP	51%	56%
EST	71%	71%
FIN	53%	51%
FRA	41%	50%
GBR	42%	56%
GRC	46%	47%
HUN	66%	70%
IDN	95%	91%
IND	86%	90%
IRL	42%	45%
ISL	42%	41%
ISR	65%	61%
ITA	46%	47%
JPN	69%	75%
KOR	43%	73%
LUX	30%	31%
LVA	67%	na
MEX	68%	91%
NLD	43%	49%
NOR	34%	32%
NZL	76%	78%
POL	67%	69%
PRT	59%	60%
RUS	100%	100%
SVK	60%	53%
SVN	42%	46%
SWE	63%	62%
TUR	75%	77%
USA	75%	83%
ZAF	89%	89%

Note: na: not available. The table includes emissions from the combustion of biomass in the emission base. Annex 3.A shows results excluding emissions from the combustion of biomass in the emission base.

The carbon pricing gap at EUR 60 was 85% on aggregate for 2015, 3 percentage points lower than in 2012. The simple unweighted average of the carbon pricing gap at EUR 60 is 69% across all countries. It decreased by three percentage points compared to 2012.

The carbon pricing gap at EUR 60 varied significantly, between 30% and 100% across countries. Few countries priced a significant share of emissions above EUR 60 outside the road sector, as Section 4.1 has shown. This means that the carbon pricing gap at EUR 60 in 2015 depended to a significant extent on how fuels in the road sector were priced and what share of total emissions of a country stem from the road sector. Still, emissions priced below EUR 60 contribute to a lower carbon pricing gap at EUR 60.

As explained in the introduction, EUR 60 per tonne of CO_2 is a midpoint estimate of carbon costs in 2020, as well as a low-end estimate of carbon costs in 2030, according to the High Level Commission on Carbon Pricing (2017[3]). While at least some countries have already advanced substantially to closing their carbon pricing gap at EUR 30, much more needs to be done for closing the gap at EUR 60 in the years to come.

Table 3.8. Carbon pricing gap at EUR 60 in 2015

Country	2015	2012
ARG	76%	na
AUS	79%	80%
AUT	62%	63%
BEL	71%	71%
BRA	97%	94%
CAN	81%	na
CHE	30%	42%
CHL	85%	88%
CHN	90%	94%
CZE	78%	79%
DEU	67%	67%
DNK	60%	48%
ESP	61%	66%
EST	80%	80%
FIN	62%	61%
FRA	52%	58%
GBR	56%	64%
GRC	60%	63%
HUN	72%	76%
IDN	97%	95%
IND	89%	94%
IRL	55%	56%
ISL	52%	49%
ISR	69%	65%
ITA	54%	54%
JPN	74%	79%
KOR	64%	80%
LUX	33%	35%
LVA	72%	na
MEX	69%	95%
NLD	54%	56%
NOR	38%	45%
NZL	78%	80%
POL	76%	78%
PRT	67%	67%
RUS	100%	100%
SVK	69%	64%
SVN	48%	56%
SWE	69%	70%
TUR	78%	80%
USA	88%	91%
ZAF	89%	89%

Note: na: not available. The table includes emissions from the combustion of biomass in the emission base. Annex 3.A shows results excluding emissions from the combustion of biomass in the emission base.

Carbon pricing – a bigger picture

Carbon prices vary significantly across countries and sectors. This section relates the extent to which countries price carbon emissions, as measured by the carbon pricing gap, to some general macro-economic variables to gain a better understanding of patterns in how countries price carbon emissions.

Figure 3.3 shows that less populous countries tend to have a smaller carbon pricing gap than more populous countries. To the extent that larger countries emit more carbon emissions than smaller ones, this pattern helps to explain findings in the preceding section that on aggregate the carbon pricing gap is large. While some countries price a significant share of their emissions at non-negligible rates, their impact on aggregate numbers is generally limited when their share in overall emissions is low.

The current pattern may soon change with introduction of the Chinese national ETS, see Chapter 2. Once China prices a large share of its emissions significantly, the aggregate carbon pricing gap will decline substantially (see also Chapter 2).

Some fairly populous countries have recently started to decrease their carbon pricing gap as described in the previous sections. The recent carbon pricing efforts by Mexico, France, the United Kingdom and Canada also contribute significantly to lowering the aggregate gap.

Figure 3.3. Less populous countries have a smaller carbon pricing gap

Carbon pricing gap at EUR 30 and population (in millions) in 2015

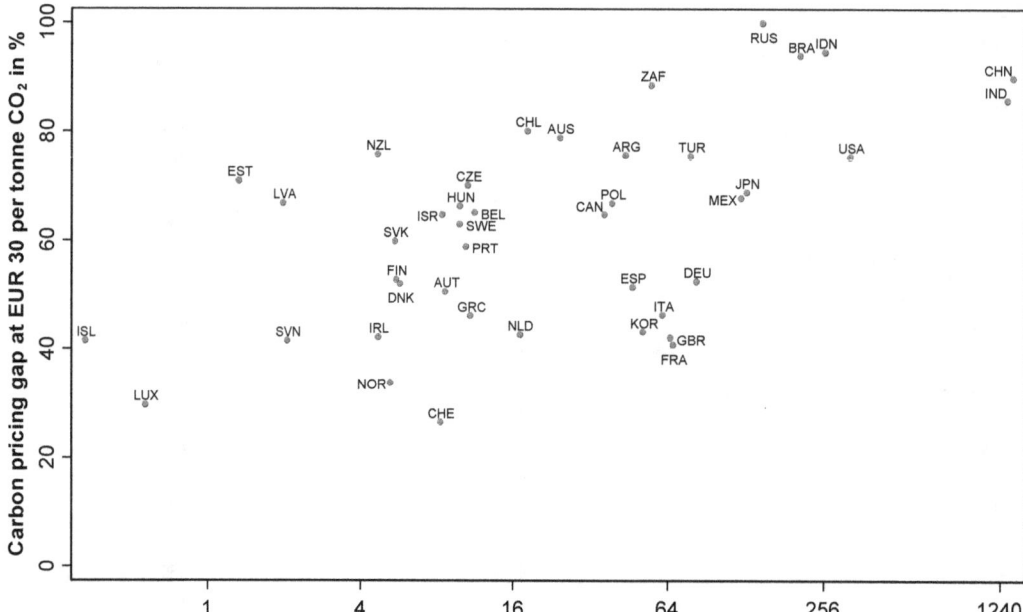

Source: Population data from OECD (2018[21]) and the World Development Indicators (World Bank, 2018[22]).

Figure 3.4 shows the carbon intensity of countries' energy uses and the energy intensity of countries' GDPs. Multiplying the carbon intensity of energy, $\frac{CO_2\ emissions}{energy\ use}$, with the energy intensity of GDP, $\frac{energy\ use}{GDP}$, gives the carbon intensity of GDP, $\frac{CO_2\ emissions}{GDP}$. Carbon intensities decrease towards the origin, i.e., the lower left corner of the graph.

Reaching the goal of the Paris Agreement to limit global temperature increase to well below 2°C requires net zero carbon emissions in the second half of this century. Scenarios congruent with the Paris Agreement by Peters et al. (2017[23]) show net zero carbon emissions for the World economy in the 2060s.[3] Net zero emissions imply that either the carbon intensity of energy is zero, the energy intensity of GDP is zero, or both, as shown by the small diamonds on the vertical and horizontal axis of Figure 3.4. While zero-carbon fuels already exist, it is hard to imagine that energy intensities of GDP decline towards zero. Hence, decarbonising economies implies that countries need to move towards the horizontal axis of the graph.

Figure 3.4. Countries with a low carbon pricing gap lead in decarbonising their economies

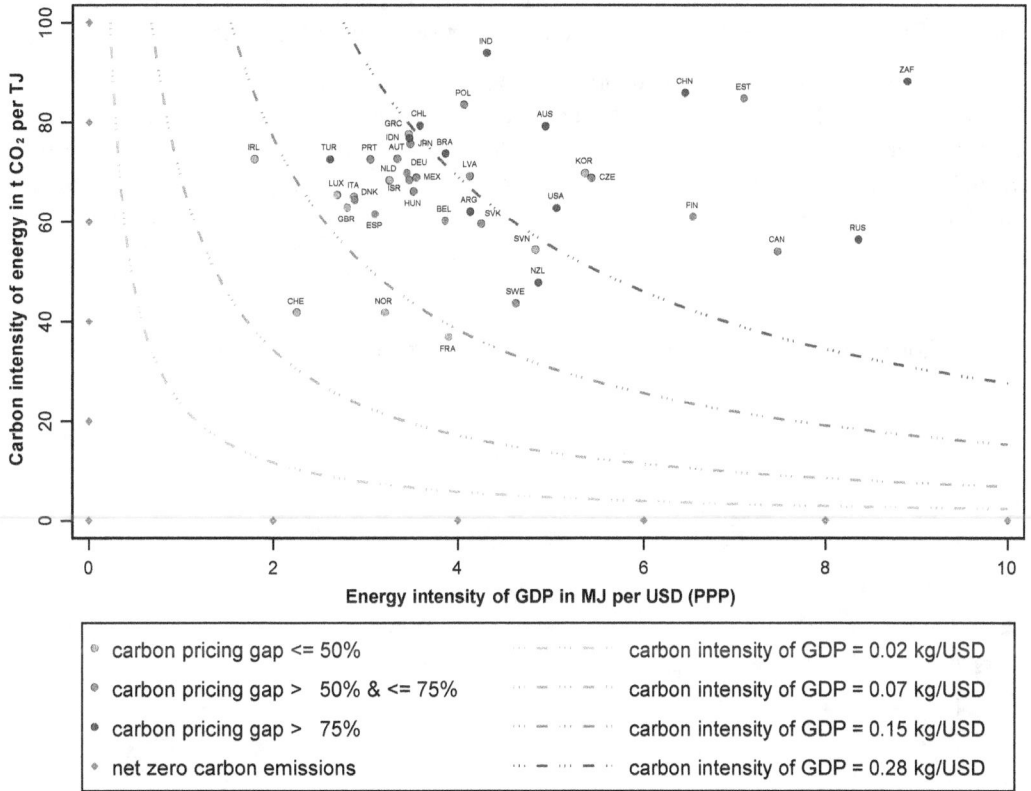

Source: GDP data from the World Development Indicators (World Bank, 2018[22]), Energy use data from the Taxing Energy Use database (OECD, 2018[1]).

Equal carbon intensities of GDP are shown by four dashed-dotted *isocarbon* lines in Figure 3.4. A lighter colour corresponds to a lower carbon intensity of GDP. The values for the *isocarbons* are based on 2°C scenarios as shown in Figure 3 of Peters et al. (2017[23]). The highest carbon intensity, 0.28 kg/USD, corresponds to the level of carbon intensity for the World economy in central scenarios in 2020. The three lighter *isocarbons* correspond to carbon intensity for the World economy in 2030, 2040 and 2050 respectively.[4]

Figure 3.4 shows that many countries have a carbon intensity below the level required in 2020 by decarbonisation pathways for reaching the 2°C goal. A considerable number of countries with a large amount of emissions are still substantially above the level of carbon intensity required in 2020 for reaching the 2°C goal. On aggregate, considerable progress needs to be made for being on track with reaching the goals of the Paris Agreement.

Countries with a low carbon pricing gap, shown by lighter colour in Figure 3.4, *tend to be more carbon-efficient*, i.e. they have a low carbon intensity of GDP. All countries emitting less than 0.15 kg CO_2 per USD in GDP have a carbon pricing gap of less than 50%. Many of the other countries with a gap below 50% show high carbon efficiencies as well.

Carbon prices raise the price of carbon-intensive energy compared to carbon-efficient energy, encouraging users to switch to more carbon-efficient fuels. Switching to more carbon-efficient fuels implies that countries move towards the horizontal axis in the graph. As long as countries use non-zero carbon fuels, carbon prices will also increase the price of energy through increasing the price of their carbon content. This encourages energy users to use less energy, making countries move towards the vertical axis.

One can expect that countries which increase and broaden carbon prices will soon improve their carbon- and energy-efficiencies. In Figure 3.4, such countries will move closer to the origin. Some countries that still had energy and carbon-intensive economies in 2015 recently broadened and increased carbon prices, among them Canada, Estonia and Korea. With their new carbon pricing efforts, one can expect that their energy- and carbon-efficiencies will improve, which will result in a movement toward the origin of Figure 3.4.

Figure 3.5. Countries with a lower carbon pricing gap are more carbon efficient

Carbon intensity of GDP and carbon pricing gap in 2015

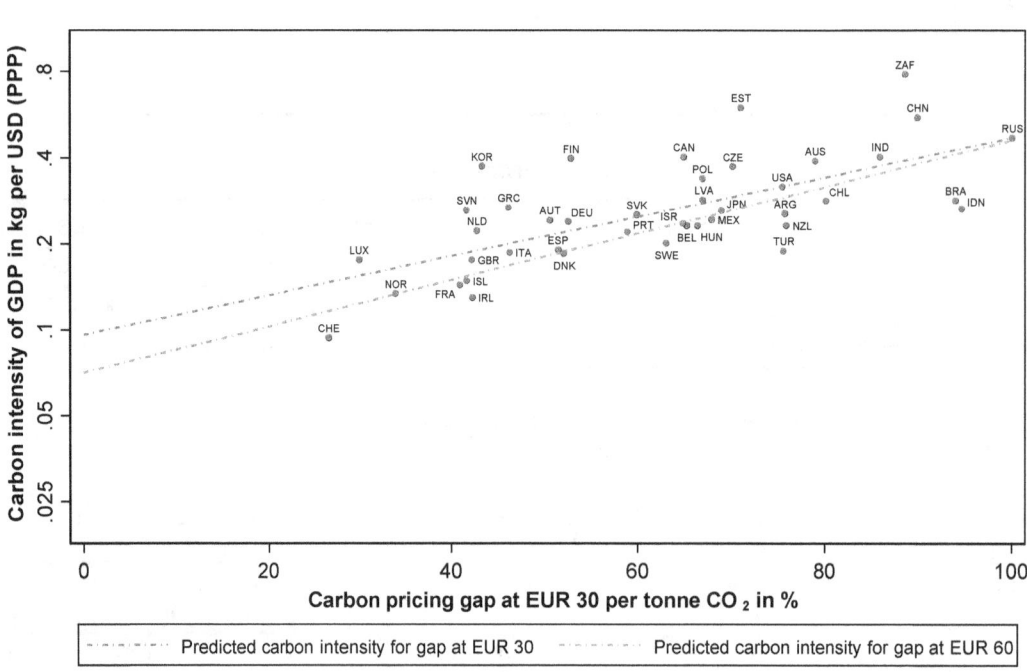

Source: GDP data from the World Development Indicators (World Bank, 2018[22]).

Figure 3.5 shows that countries with a lower carbon pricing gap are more carbon efficient, as measured by fewer carbon emissions per unit of GDP. The relationship between comprehensive carbon pricing, i.e. a low gap, and low carbon emissions does not necessarily imply a direct causal effect in either direction. Low emissions per unit of GDP can be the result of comprehensive carbon pricing steering the economy to low-emission energy sources. Alternatively, however, countries with fewer emissions per unit of GDP may find it easier to price emissions. That said, empirical evidence clearly shows that higher carbon prices discourage emissions (Arlinghaus (2015[24]), Martin et al. (2016[25])), showing in lower emissions per unit of GDP.

A simple log-linear regression of the carbon intensity of GDP on the carbon pricing gap at EUR 30 reveals that a one percentage point increase in the carbon pricing gap is associated with a 0.016 percent increase in the carbon intensity of GDP in 2015. At EUR 60, a one percentage point increase in the carbon pricing gap is associated with a 0.019 increase in the carbon intensity of GDP. A reduction of the carbon pricing gap at a higher price level thus appears to associate with a stronger decrease in emissions per GDP than the same percentage point reduction of the carbon pricing gap at a lower level.

The log-linear association between the carbon pricing gap and the carbon intensity of GDP suggests that reducing the carbon pricing gap at EUR 30 would lead to a carbon intensity of about 0.1 kg per USD of GDP. At EUR 60, a zero carbon pricing gap associates with a carbon intensity of about 0.07 kg per unit of GDP. For reaching a net zero-carbon intensity of GDP price levels will need to be higher. Over time, technological progress can also reduce the carbon intensity of GDP.

Annex 3.A. CO_2 emissions from the combustion of biomass

This Annex provides tables on how excluding emissions from biomass affects the shares of emissions priced at different levels of effective carbon rates. It starts with a discussion of how evidence on life cycle emissions from biomass supports the choice for including these emissions as the default for this report and related reports.

In line with previous editions of *Taxing Energy Use* (OECD (2013[26]), OECD (2015[27]) and OECD (2018[1])) as well as of *Effective Carbon Rates* (OECD, 2016[18]), this report includes *emissions from the combustion* of biomass in the emissions base. This means that CO_2 emissions from the combustion of biomass are treated in the same way as CO_2 emissions from the combustion of fossil fuels.

An alternative approach would be to assume that the net effect of production and consumption of biomass for fuels is *carbon neutral* as plants bind carbon from the atmosphere as they grow. Emissions from combustion of biomass would then be excluded from the emission base. The assumption of carbon neutrality from a *lifecycle* perspective has increasingly been challenged in the scientific literature (see, e.g., Fargione et al. (2008[28]), Searchinger et al, (2008[29]) and Liska et al. (2014[30])). The fifth IPCC assessment report states that the "neutrality perception [of biofuel emissions] is linked to a misunderstanding of the guidelines for GHG inventories" (Smith et al (2014, p. 879[31]), see also the penultimate paragraph of this Annex).

Searchinger et al. (2008[29]) note that the *lifecycle* approach ought to account for indirect emissions from land-use change triggered by the cultivation of biofuel crops. One potential impact is that, when biomass is planted on fields traditionally used for food production, food prices will increase. This will increase the return on agricultural land and encourages farmers to grow food on previously native land. Native land generally binds more carbon than agricultural land, and the net effect is that emissions increase. A second possible impact is that biomass for fuel production is grown on previously native land. Plants for biomass production have a shorter lifetime than native plants, meaning CO_2 is bound for a shorter period, so that emissions increase.

The upshot is that taking emissions from land-use change into account is complex and quantitative modelling shows a wide range of estimates depending on the pathways, local conditions and technologies considered.

A recent study (Ecofys, IIASA and E4tech, 2015[32]) calculates the effects of land-use change for a wide range of biofuels consumed in European countries (see also Smith et al. (2014, p. 878[31]), Figure 11.24 for an earlier review of quantitative estimates) The study finds, among other things, that lifecycle emissions of biodiesel produced from food and feedstock *on average* exceed those of fossil fuels by about 80% (Transport & Environment, 2016[33]). This average conceals large variation. For example, there are large differences across crops: biodiesel produced from palm oil emits about three times as much carbon dioxide as fossil diesel, while biodiesel produced from sunflowers emits about the same amount as fossil diesel. Bioethanol from food and feedstock (e.g. maize, wheat, barley etc.) emits on average about two thirds of the carbon emissions from fossil diesel. Only advanced non-food based biofuels (e.g. from short-rotation coppice) are found to be potentially carbon neutral. In line with these findings, the ongoing (at the time of writing) revision of the European Directive on renewable energy (European Parliament and the Council, 2009[34]) which will update the Directive for the 2030 EU climate and energy goals, may no longer contain any target for biofuels. Instead a cap on biofuels produced from food and feedstock at 7% is being considered.

The present report calculates its emission base from the Extended World Energy Balances (EWEB) produced by the International Energy Agency (IEA, 2017[2]) as described in in Annex A of OECD (2016[18]). EWEB does not specify the source or the origins of biofuels, i.e. whether rape, soy, maize or some other input has been used to produce biofuels and where the inputs have been grown. This lack of evidence makes estimates of the lifecycle impact of biofuels more uncertain.

One indication can be extracted from one of the main scenarios of the joint ECOFYS, IASSA and E4tech (2015[32]) study, which assumes a 7% cap on biofuels produced from food and feedstock. In this scenario, overall biofuel consumption in 2020 consists of 60% biodiesel (which on average emits 80% more CO_2 than fossil diesel) and 20% bioethanol (which emits two-thirds of the emissions from fossil diesel). Given this mix, overall biofuel lifecycle emissions would be close to those of fossil diesel, and would be more likely to exceed than fall below emissions from fossil diesel. Against this background, the "combustion approach" to emissions taken in *Taxing Energy Use* (OECD (2013[26]) and *Effective Carbon Rates* (OECD, 2016[18]) may also be regarded as informative about *lifecycle* emissions. Of course, conditions may differ across countries and across time, but in-depth analysis of the life cycle emissions from biofuels at the country level is well beyond the scope of this report.

Taxing Energy Use (OECD (2013[26]), OECD (2015[27]) and OECD (2018[1])) and *Effective Carbon Rates* (OECD, 2016[18]) calculate emissions from energy use directly from the IEA's (2017[2]) EWEB as this database provides timely and consistent yearly data by fuel and user for all 42 OECD and G20 economies included in the study. By comparison, UNFCCC Greenhouse Gas inventories also cover emission sources beyond energy use (industrial process emissions as well as emissions from agriculture, forestry and other land use) and non-CO_2 greenhouse gas emissions. UNFCCC greenhouse gas inventories are more difficult to compare across countries than the IEA's EWEB as countries have significant leeway on how to report emissions. As a result, emission bases from *Taxing Energy Use* (OECD (2013[26]) and *Effective Carbon Rates* (OECD, 2016[18]) are not directly comparable with those from UNFCCC inventories.

In addition to the abovementioned differences, UNFCCC inventories account for emissions from biomass not in the category for emission from energy use, but in a different category, namely for emissions from agriculture, forestry and other land use (IPCC, 2008[35]). The present report only considers emissions from energy use, so it cannot account for emissions induced by the use of biofuels in a separate category for agriculture, forestry and other land use. The combustion approach taken here may nevertheless be informative about lifecycle emissions of biofuels as mentioned above.

The above considerations support the adoption of the *combustion approach* as the default for presenting results in this report. Nevertheless, the alternative assumption (neutrality from a life cycle perspective) may be of interest to specific countries or users, as it may better reflect local conditions or improve comparability with other inventories. Therefore, this annex provides tables showing results *excluding* emissions from the combustion of biomass. These tables can be described as showing the share of priced emissions at different levels of effective carbon rates if all biofuels used were carbon neutral. By providing this second benchmark, readers can also draw inferences on how results change given specific information about the lifecycle emissions from biofuels.

Annex Table 3.A.1. Proportion of emissions priced per tonne of CO_2 by country

Excluding emissions from the combustion of biomass in the emission base

	EUR 0	EUR 5	EUR 30	EUR 60
ARG	76%	26%	26%	22%
AUS	24%	24%	22%	21%
AUT	83%	83%	46%	34%
BEL	80%	71%	26%	26%
BRA	46%	41%	0%	0%
CAN	65%	65%	17%	0%
CHE	96%	91%	84%	43%
CHL	27%	27%	27%	12%
CHN	22%	9%	9%	9%
CZE	89%	76%	17%	17%
DEU	97%	96%	21%	20%
DNK	98%	98%	47%	46%
ESP	94%	92%	37%	30%
EST	87%	84%	16%	13%
FIN	96%	96%	68%	52%
FRA	94%	94%	47%	39%
GBR	81%	80%	53%	29%
GRC	97%	97%	33%	27%
HUN	80%	77%	27%	27%
IDN	25%	25%	0%	0%
IND	88%	22%	13%	3%
IRL	97%	97%	37%	30%
ISL	80%	80%	39%	39%
ISR	98%	29%	27%	27%
ITA	99%	98%	45%	41%
JPN	86%	40%	21%	19%
KOR	98%	98%	17%	16%
LUX	99%	88%	66%	65%
LVA	92%	89%	45%	42%
MEX	65%	35%	33%	33%
NLD	97%	97%	39%	35%
NOR	93%	92%	69%	63%
NZL	87%	23%	23%	22%
POL	91%	81%	16%	16%
PRT	95%	93%	35%	32%
RUS	35%	0%	0%	0%
SVK	87%	75%	30%	18%
SVN	100%	100%	56%	51%
SWE	96%	96%	57%	56%
TUR	51%	24%	22%	21%
USA	38%	38%	4%	0%
ZAF	14%	13%	13%	11%

Annex Table 3.A.2. Proportion of emissions priced in the electricity sector per tonne of CO_2 by country

Excluding emissions from the combustion of biomass in the emission base

Country	Proportion of emissions priced at or above in 2015			
	EUR 0	EUR 5	EUR 30	EUR 60
ARG	74%	13%	13%	0%
AUS	0%	0%	0%	0%
AUT	100%	100%	0%	0%
BEL	90%	89%	0%	0%
BRA	10%	10%	0%	0%
CAN	55%	55%	0%	0%
CHE	75%	75%	75%	0%
CHL	0%	0%	0%	0%
CHN	14%	0%	0%	0%
CZE	100%	100%	0%	0%
DEU	100%	100%	0%	0%
DNK	100%	100%	0%	0%
ESP	100%	100%	0%	0%
EST	92%	92%	0%	0%
FIN	100%	100%	0%	0%
FRA	100%	100%	0%	0%
GBR	100%	100%	90%	0%
GRC	100%	100%	12%	2%
HUN	100%	100%	0%	0%
IDN	0%	0%	0%	0%
IND	98%	0%	0%	0%
IRL	100%	100%	0%	0%
ISL	0%	0%	0%	0%
ISR	100%	1%	1%	1%
ITA	100%	100%	0%	0%
JPN	91%	13%	0%	0%
KOR	100%	100%	0%	0%
LUX	77%	77%	0%	0%
LVA	100%	100%	0%	0%
MEX	47%	1%	1%	1%
NLD	100%	100%	0%	0%
NOR	100%	100%	0%	0%
NZL	84%	0%	0%	0%
POL	100%	100%	0%	0%
PRT	100%	100%	0%	0%
RUS	0%	0%	0%	0%
SVK	100%	100%	0%	0%
SVN	100%	100%	0%	0%
SWE	100%	100%	0%	0%
TUR	32%	0%	0%	0%
USA	8%	8%	0%	0%
ZAF	0%	0%	0%	0%

Annex Table 3.A.3. Proportion of emissions priced in the industry sector per tonne of CO_2 by country

Excluding emissions from the combustion of biomass in the emission base

Country	Proportion of emissions priced at or above in 2015			
	EUR 0	EUR 5	EUR 30	EUR 60
ARG	65%	2%	2%	1%
AUS	3%	3%	3%	3%
AUT	64%	64%	16%	4%
BEL	64%	62%	0%	0%
BRA	19%	4%	0%	0%
CAN	58%	58%	0%	0%
CHE	88%	63%	29%	1%
CHL	0%	0%	0%	0%
CHN	17%	2%	2%	1%
CZE	91%	52%	0%	0%
DEU	90%	87%	1%	0%
DNK	98%	98%	21%	16%
ESP	80%	74%	5%	0%
EST	67%	56%	5%	0%
FIN	94%	94%	70%	46%
FRA	85%	85%	2%	0%
GBR	84%	83%	9%	5%
GRC	98%	96%	17%	5%
HUN	83%	72%	4%	4%
IDN	0%	0%	0%	0%
IND	83%	24%	2%	0%
IRL	83%	83%	3%	0%
ISL	24%	24%	0%	0%
ISR	85%	6%	0%	0%
ITA	99%	98%	2%	2%
JPN	70%	32%	5%	5%
KOR	99%	99%	2%	2%
LUX	100%	86%	0%	0%
LVA	93%	85%	0%	0%
MEX	42%	4%	4%	4%
NLD	90%	90%	16%	3%
NOR	90%	89%	52%	52%
NZL	74%	2%	2%	0%
POL	99%	71%	2%	2%
PRT	88%	79%	5%	0%
RUS	44%	0%	0%	0%
SVK	78%	60%	13%	0%
SVN	99%	99%	48%	47%
SWE	93%	93%	13%	11%
TUR	41%	13%	4%	0%
USA	8%	8%	0%	0%
ZAF	5%	5%	5%	1%

Annex Table 3.A.4. Proportion of emissions priced in the residential and commercial sector per tonne of CO_2 by country

Excluding emissions from the combustion of biomass in the emission base

Country	Proportion of emissions priced at or above in 2015			
	EUR 0	EUR 5	EUR 30	EUR 60
ARG	99%	1%	1%	0%
AUS	1%	1%	1%	1%
AUT	100%	100%	47%	0%
BEL	81%	48%	0%	0%
BRA	0%	0%	0%	0%
CAN	29%	29%	0%	0%
CHE	99%	99%	99%	0%
CHL	8%	8%	0%	0%
CHN	14%	9%	9%	9%
CZE	25%	24%	0%	0%
DEU	100%	98%	1%	1%
DNK	99%	99%	76%	76%
ESP	100%	99%	33%	0%
EST	90%	88%	24%	1%
FIN	99%	99%	99%	98%
FRA	97%	97%	35%	0%
GBR	29%	29%	4%	0%
GRC	99%	99%	16%	14%
HUN	33%	33%	1%	1%
IDN	0%	0%	0%	0%
IND	29%	0%	0%	0%
IRL	100%	100%	23%	0%
ISL	100%	100%	0%	0%
ISR	100%	100%	0%	0%
ITA	100%	100%	76%	67%
JPN	100%	64%	31%	18%
KOR	94%	94%	17%	13%
LUX	100%	50%	0%	0%
LVA	92%	84%	2%	2%
MEX	89%	2%	2%	2%
NLD	99%	99%	99%	99%
NOR	100%	100%	100%	88%
NZL	93%	5%	5%	0%
POL	41%	31%	0%	0%
PRT	100%	100%	15%	12%
RUS	8%	0%	0%	0%
SVK	96%	87%	29%	0%
SVN	100%	100%	55%	0%
SWE	98%	98%	98%	98%
TUR	56%	5%	5%	4%
USA	5%	5%	0%	0%
ZAF	6%	1%	1%	1%

Annex Table 3.A.5. Proportion of emissions priced in the road transport sector per tonne of CO_2 by country

Excluding emissions from the combustion of biomass in the emission base

Country	Proportion of emissions priced at or above in 2015			
	EUR 0	EUR 5	EUR 30	EUR 60
ARG	100%	100%	100%	100%
AUS	100%	100%	100%	96%
AUT	100%	100%	100%	100%
BEL	99%	99%	99%	99%
BRA	83%	83%	0%	0%
CAN	100%	100%	67%	0%
CHE	100%	100%	100%	100%
CHL	100%	100%	100%	43%
CHN	94%	94%	94%	94%
CZE	100%	100%	100%	98%
DEU	100%	100%	100%	100%
DNK	100%	100%	100%	100%
ESP	100%	100%	99%	99%
EST	100%	100%	100%	100%
FIN	100%	100%	100%	100%
FRA	100%	100%	100%	100%
GBR	100%	100%	100%	100%
GRC	100%	100%	100%	100%
HUN	100%	100%	100%	100%
IDN	100%	100%	0%	0%
IND	98%	98%	98%	29%
IRL	100%	100%	100%	100%
ISL	100%	100%	100%	100%
ISR	100%	100%	100%	100%
ITA	100%	98%	98%	98%
JPN	100%	100%	100%	98%
KOR	100%	100%	97%	97%
LUX	100%	100%	100%	100%
LVA	100%	100%	100%	94%
MEX	100%	98%	98%	98%
NLD	100%	100%	100%	100%
NOR	100%	100%	100%	100%
NZL	100%	55%	55%	54%
POL	100%	100%	100%	100%
PRT	100%	100%	100%	100%
RUS	99%	0%	0%	0%
SVK	100%	100%	100%	100%
SVN	100%	100%	100%	99%
SWE	100%	100%	100%	100%
TUR	100%	100%	100%	100%
USA	100%	100%	10%	0%
ZAF	100%	100%	100%	100%

Annex Table 3.A.6. Carbon pricing gap at EUR 30 in 2015

Excluding emissions from the combustion of biomass in the emission base

Country	Carbon pricing gap at EUR 30
ARG	74%
AUS	78%
AUT	33%
BEL	61%
BRA	90%
CAN	62%
CHE	13%
CHL	73%
CHN	89%
CZE	66%
DEU	48%
DNK	31%
ESP	47%
EST	65%
FIN	25%
FRA	32%
GBR	38%
GRC	42%
HUN	58%
IDN	92%
IND	80%
IRL	40%
ISL	40%
ISR	65%
ITA	39%
JPN	68%
KOR	42%
LUX	28%
LVA	39%
MEX	65%
NLD	41%
NOR	25%
NZL	72%
POL	64%
PRT	49%
RUS	100%
SVK	55%
SVN	29%
SWE	24%
TUR	75%
USA	75%
ZAF	87%

Annex Table 3.A.7. Carbon pricing gap at EUR 60 in 2015

Excluding emissions from the combustion of biomass in the emission base

Country	Carbon pricing gap at EUR 60
ARG	75%
AUS	78%
AUT	47%
BEL	68%
BRA	95%
CAN	80%
CHE	17%
CHL	79%
CHN	90%
CZE	74%
DEU	64%
DNK	43%
ESP	58%
EST	75%
FIN	30%
FRA	45%
GBR	53%
GRC	57%
HUN	65%
IDN	96%
IND	84%
IRL	54%
ISL	51%
ISR	69%
ITA	48%
JPN	74%
KOR	63%
LUX	31%
LVA	47%
MEX	66%
NLD	52%
NOR	30%
NZL	75%
POL	74%
PRT	58%
RUS	100%
SVK	65%
SVN	37%
SWE	34%
TUR	77%
USA	87%
ZAF	87%

Notes

[1] Tax rates and permit prices are reported in 2015 price levels.

[2] Quemin and Trotignon (2018[92]) predict that permit prices will increase moderately to about EUR 38 per tonne CO_2 in absence of any major economic shock. In case of an economic crisis permit prices are expected to trade at about EUR 10.

[3] Net carbon emissions become negative from the 2060, meaning that the amount of emissions removed from the atmosphere need to be larger than the amount of emissions emitted.

[4] In line with recent data (OECD, 2016[18]) it is assumed that carbon emission from energy use account for 69% of total greenhouse gas emissions in 2020. Many scenarios assume that the energy use decarbonises faster than other sectors, e.g. agriculture or industrial processes (European Commission, 2011[93]). Therefore it also assumed that the share of energy use in total greenhouse gas emissions declines by one percentage point a year from 2020 onwards.

References

Arlinghaus, J. (2015), "Impacts of Carbon Prices on Indicators of Competitiveness: A Review of Empirical Findings", *OECD Environment Working Papers*, No. 87, OECD Publishing, Paris, http://dx.doi.org/10.1787/5js37p21grzq-en. [24]

Arlinghaus, J. and K. Van Dender (2017), "The environmental tax and subsidy reform in Mexico", *OECD Taxation Working Papers*, No. 31, OECD Publishing, Paris, http://dx.doi.org/10.1787/a9204f40-en. [4]

Ecofys, IIASA and E4tech (2015), *The land use change impact of biofuels consumed in the EU: Quantification of area and greenhosue gas impacts*, Ecofys, IIASA and E4tech. [32]

Enerdata (2018), "Aligning the climate and energy framework to meet EU long-term climate ambition", http://www.leonardo-energy.org/resources/1362/aligning-the-climate-and-energy-framework-to-meet-eu-long-te-5a82f1469befc (accessed on 19 April 2018). [13]

European Commission (2011), *A Roadmap for moving to a competitive low carbon economy in 2050*, http://eur-lex.europa.eu/legal-content/EN/TXT/PDF/?uri=CELEX:52011DC0112&from=EN (accessed on 20 April 2018). [37]

European Energy Exchange (2015), *Emission Spot Primary Market Auction Report 2015*, European Energy Exchange, Leipzig, https://www.eex.com/de/marktdaten/umweltprodukte/auktionsmarkt/european-emission-allowances-auction/european-emission-allowances-auction-download (accessed on 23 March 2018). [7]

European Parliament and the Council (2009), *Directive 2009/28/EC of the European Parliament and of the Council of 23 April 2009 on the promotion of the use of energy from renewable sources and amending and subsequently repealing Directives 2001/77/EC and 2003/30/EC (Text with EEA relevance)*, https://eur-lex.europa.eu/legal-content/EN/ALL/?uri=CELEX:32009L0028 (accessed on 01 June 2018). [34]

European Union (2018), "Directive (EU) 2018/ 410 of the European Parliament and the Council - of 14 March 2018 - amending Directive 2003/ 87/ EC to enhance cost-effective emission reductions and low-carbon investments, and Decision (EU) 2015/ 1814", *Official Journal of the European Union*, Vol. 1933/76, http://eur-lex.europa.eu/legal-content/EN/TXT/PDF/?uri=CELEX:32018L0410&from=EN (accessed on 19 April 2018). [12]

Fargione, J. et al. (2008), "Land clearing and the biofuel carbon debt.", *Science (New York, N.Y.)*, Vol. 319/5867, pp. 1235-8, http://dx.doi.org/10.1126/science.1152747. [28]

Flues, F. and K. Van Dender (2017), "Permit allocation rules and investment incentives in emissions trading systems", *OECD Taxation Working Papers*, No. 33, OECD Publishing, Paris, http://dx.doi.org/10.1787/c3acf05e-en. [14]

Hausfather, Z. (2018), *Analysis: UK carbon emissions in 2017 fell to levels last seen in 1890 | Carbon Brief*, Carbon Brief, https://www.carbonbrief.org/analysis-uk-carbon-emissions-in-2017-fell-to-levels-last-seen-in-1890 (accessed on 19 April 2018). [10]

High-Level Commission on Carbon Prices (2017), *Report of the High-Level Commission on Carbon Prices*, World Bank, Washington, D.C., https://static1.squarespace.com/static/54ff9c5ce4b0a53decccfb4c/t/59b7f2409f8dce5316811916/1505227332748/CarbonPricing_FullReport.pdf (accessed on 16 February 2018). [3]

Hirst, D. (2018), "Carbon Price Floor (CPF) and the price support mechanism", *Briefing Paper*, No. 05927, House of Commons Library, London. [6]

IEA (2017), *Extended World Energy Balances*, http://www.iea.org/statistics/topics/energybalances. [2]

IPCC (2008), *IPCC Guidelines for National Greenhouse Gas Inventories – A primer, Prepared by the National Greenhouse Gas Inventories Programme*, IGES, Hayama, Japan, http://www.ipcc-nggip.iges.or.jp (accessed on 01 June 2018). [35]

Le Conseil fédéral suisse (2015), *Objectif de réduction 2014 manqué: hausse de la taxe CO2 sur les combustibles en 2016*, Confédération suisse, Berne, https://www.admin.ch/gov/fr/accueil/documentation/communiques.msg-id-58016.html (accessed on 12 March 2018). [17]

Le Conseil fédéral suisse (2013), *Objectif de réduction 2012 non tenu: hausse de la taxe CO2 sur les combustibles dès 2014*, Confédération suisse, Berne, https://www.admin.ch/gov/fr/accueil/documentation/communiques.msg-id-49576.html (accessed on 12 March 2018). [16]

Liska, A. et al. (2014), "Biofuels from crop residue can reduce soil carbon and increase CO_2 emissions", *Nature Climate Change*, Vol. 4/5, pp. 398-401, http://dx.doi.org/10.1038/nclimate2187. [30]

Martin, R., M. Muûls and U. Wagner (2016), "The Impact of the European Union Emissions Trading Scheme on Regulated Firms: What Is the Evidence after Ten Years?", *Review of Environmental Economics and Policy*, Vol. 10/1, pp. 129-148, http://dx.doi.org/10.1093/reep/rev016. [25]

Ministère de la Transition écologique et solidaire de la République Francaise (2018), *Fiscalité des énergies*, https://www.ecologique-solidaire.gouv.fr/fiscalite-des-energies (accessed on 12 March 2018). [15]

OECD (2018), *OECD.Stat, Population*, OECD, Paris, http://stats.oecd.org/ (accessed on 15 February 2018). [21]

OECD (2018), *Taxing Energy Use 2018: Companion to the Taxing Energy Use Database*, OECD Publishing, Paris. [1]

OECD (2016), *Effective Carbon Rates: Pricing CO2 through Taxes and Emissions Trading Systems*, OECD Publishing, Paris, http://dx.doi.org/10.1787/9789264260115-en. [18]

OECD (2015), *Taxing Energy Use 2015: OECD and Selected Partner Economies*, OECD Publishing, Paris, http://dx.doi.org/10.1787/9789264232334-en. [27]

OECD (2013), *Taxing Energy Use: A Graphical Analysis*, OECD Publishing, Paris, http://dx.doi.org/10.1787/9789264183933-en. [26]

Peters, G. et al. (2017), "Key indicators to track current progress and future ambition of the Paris Agreement", *Nature Climate Change*, Vol. 7/2, pp. 118-122, http://dx.doi.org/10.1038/nclimate3202. [23]

Quemin, S. and R. Trotignon (2018), *European carbon market: Impacts of the reform and stability reserve until 2030*, Dauphine Université Paris, Paris. [36]

Santos, G. (2017), "Road fuel taxes in Europe: Do they internalize road transport externalities?", *Transport Policy*, Vol. 53, pp. 120-134, http://dx.doi.org/10.1016/J.TRANPOL.2016.09.009. [20]

Searchinger, T. et al. (2008), "Use of U.S. croplands for biofuels increases greenhouse gases through emissions from land-use change.", *Science (New York, N.Y.)*, Vol. 319/5867, pp. 1238-40, http://dx.doi.org/10.1126/science.1151861. [29]

Smith, P. et al. (2014), "Agriculture, Forestry and Other Land Use (AFOLU)", in Edenhofer, O. et al. (eds.), *Climate Change 2014: Mitigation of Climate Change. Contribution of Working Group III to the Fifth Assessment Report of the Intergovernmental Panel on Climate Change*, Cambridge University Press, Cambridge, United Kingdom and New York, NY, USA.. [31]

South African Treasury (2015), *National assembly question for written reply. Question Number 2360 [NW2772E]*, http://www.treasury.gov.za/publications/other/MinAnsw/2015/Reply%20to%20PQ%202360%20%5bNW2722E%5d.pdf (accessed on 19 April 2018). [5]

Transport & Environment (2016), *Globiom: the basis for biofuel policy post-2020*, Transport & Environment, Brussels, Belgium, https://www.transportenvironment.org/sites/te/files/publications/2016_04_TE_Globiom_paper_FINAL_0.pdf (accessed on 01 June 2018). [33]

UK Department for Business Energy & Industrial Strategy (2018), *Updated energy and emissions projection 2017*, Crown, London, https://www.gov.uk/government/publications/updated-energy-and-emissions-projections-2017. [9]

UK Department for Business, E. (2017), *National Statistics: Digest of UK Energy Statistics (DUKES): Fuel used in generation (DUKES 5.3)*, https://www.gov.uk/government/statistics/electricity-chapter-5-digest-of-united-kingdom-energy-statistics-dukes (accessed on 27 February 2018). [8]

Van Dender, K. (2018), "Taxing vehicles, fuel, and road use: what mix for road transport?", *forthcoming in: OECD Taxation Working Papers*, OECD Publishing, Paris. [19]

Ward, A. (2018), "Coal's rapid decline drives carbon emissions down to 1890 levels", *Financial Times*, https://www.ft.com/content/47563b2a-21f6-11e8-9a70-08f715791301. [11]

World Bank (2018), *World Development Indicators (WDI)*, The World Bank, https://datacatalog.worldbank.org/dataset/world-development-indicators (accessed on 15 February 2018). [22]

Annex A. Description of emissions trading systems and results

Annex A.1 describes the seventeen emission trading systems and tradeable performance standards for which coverage and permit prices were estimated in 2015: The Alberta Specified Gas Emitters Regulation and the Quebec Cap-and-Trade System in Canada, the seven Chinese pilot systems (Beijing, Chongqing, Guangdong, Hubei, Shanghai, Shenzhen, Tianjin), the European Union Emissions Trading System, the systems in Saitama and Tokyo (Japan), Korea, New Zealand, Switzerland, and the California Cap-and-Trade Program as well as the Regional Greenhouse Gas Initiative in the United States. Annex A.2 shows results on ETS and tradeable performance standard coverage by sector and permit prices. Annex A.3 lists the system-specific adjustment and assumptions for the calculations.

A.1. Description of emissions trading systems used in the analysis

Table A.1 summarises the main features of the seventeen emissions trading systems and tradeable performance standards that were operational in 2015. These carbon pricing systems are included in the estimation of effective carbon rates as presented in Chapter 3 on carbon pricing developments. Regarding recent carbon pricing trends (Chapter 2) Table 2.1 lists all new carbon pricing systems, which have become operational since 2016 or are expected to become operational soon, and are included in the forward-looking estimates of Chapter 2.

ANNEX A: DESCRIPTION OF EMISSIONS TRADING SYSTEMS AND RESULTS | 77

Table A.1. Description of emissions trading systems used in the analysis

Country or region	Juris-dictions covered	Date trading started	Year used in the estimation	Greenhouse gas emissions covered	Sectors and activities covered	Threshold for inclusion of emitting facility (per year)	Number of facilities	Price Ceiling or Floor	Treatment of biomass
CAN	Alberta	July 2007	2015	CO_2, CH_4, N_2O, SF_6, HFCs, PFCs, NF_3	- Main industrial facilities, including pipelines, - Electricity generation & imports	100,000 tCO_2-eq	121 (estimate)	Permit prices are set to CAD 15 in 2015, determined by ministerial order.	Not covered
	Quebec	January 2013	2015		- Main industrial facilities, including pipelines, - Electricity generation & imports, - Fuel suppliers	25,000 tCO_2-eq	76	- Price floor: CAD 10.75 (2013), increasing annually by 5% plus rate of inflation - Price ceiling: release of allowances from reserve account at CAD 40, 45 and 50 (2013); ceilings increase annually by 5% and are adjusted for inflation (Gouvernement du Québec, 2017[1])	Not covered
CHN	Beijing	Nov 2013	2015 (partial)	CO_2	- Electricity & heat generation, - Industries, - Services	10,000 tCO_2	490		
	Chongqing	June 2014	2015 (partial)	CO_2, CH_4, N_2O, HFCs, PFCs, SF_6	- Electricity & heat generation, - Industries	20,000 tCO_2-eq	242		
	Guangdong	Dec 2013	2015 (partial)	CO_2	- Electricity & heat generation, - Industries	20,000 tCO_2	202		
	Hubei	April 2014	2015 (partial)	CO_2	- Electricity & heat generation, - Industries	15,000 tCO_2	138		
	Shanghai	Nov 2013	2015 (partial)	CO_2	- Electricity & heat generation, - Industries, - Services	20,000 tCO_2	191		
	Shenzhen	June 2013	2015 (partial)	CO_2	- Electricity & heat generation, - Water supply, - Manufacturing,	5,000 tCO_2	635 (+197 public buildings)		

ANNEX A: DESCRIPTION OF EMISSIONS TRADING SYSTEMS AND RESULTS

	Region	Start date	Coverage	Gases	Sectors	Threshold	Market stabilisation measures	Number of entities	Offsets
	Tianjin	Dec 2013	2015 (partial)	CO_2	- Buildings - Power & heat generation, - Industries	20,000 tCO_2		114	No need to surrender permits
EU	23 countries	Jan 2005	2015	CO_2, N_2O, PFCs	- Energy activities, - Ferrous metal, - Cement, glass and ceramics, - Pulp and paper - Aviation	Depends on activity, e.g. 20 MW thermal input for combustion activities, see European Commission (2003, Annex I) for details		>11000	
JPN	Tokyo	April 2010	2015	CO_2	Large commercial and industrial facilities	1,500 kl energy in crude oil equivalents	None	about 1300	No need to surrender permits
	Saitama	April 2011	2015	CO_2			None	608	No need to surrender permits
KOR	National	Jan 2015	2015	CO_2, CH_4, N_2O, HFCs, PFCs, SF_6	- Electricity generation, - Manufacturing, - Water supply, - Waste & sewerage, - Construction, - Air transport (5 airlines)	125,000 tCO_2-eq (companies) 25,000 tCO_2-eq (installations)	President can enact market stabilisation measures (price ceiling and floor, additional release of permits)	525	No need to surrender permits
NZL	National	Jan 2008 (extended to more sectors in following years)	2015	CO_2, CH_4, N_2O, HFCs, PFCs, SF_6	- Liquid fuel suppliers, - Stationary energy (gas and coal for electricity & heat generation), - Industrial processes (metal, mineral and chemical transformation), - Disposal facility operators, - Horticulture, - Primary industries (agriculture, forestry), - Synthetic GHG	Upstream coverage for each sector	- Mandatory participants can surrender one permit for every two tonnes of emissions. - Price ceiling: NZD 12.5 (half of NZD 25 due to the one-for-two transitional measure)	109[1]	Not covered
CHE	National	Jan 2008	2015	CO_2, CH_4, N_2O, HFCs,	- Non-metallic minerals, metal & steel production	20 MW (installed total rated thermal)		54	No need to surrender

ANNEX A: DESCRIPTION OF EMISSIONS TRADING SYSTEMS AND RESULTS | 79

							permits
		PFCs, SF$_6$, NF$_3$	- Chemicals & pharmaceuticals, - Paper production, - District heating, - Refineries	input) or sector-specific criteria, see Swiss Federal Council, Annex 6 (2012)[2]			Not covered
USA California	Jan 2013	CO$_2$, CH$_4$, N$_2$O, SF$_6$, HFCs, PFCs, NF$_3$	- Main industrial facilities, - Electricity generation & imports, - CO2 suppliers, - Fuel supplier	25,000 tCO2-eq	416	- Price floor: USD 10 in 2012, increasing annually by 5% plus rate of inflation, - Price ceiling: release of allowances from reserve account at USD 40, 45 and 50	
RGGI	Jan 2009	CO$_2$	Electricity generation	25 MW (installed capacity)	161		Not covered[2]

Note: [1]This number refers to the number of participants with activities registered in the New Zealand Emissions Trading System up to end 2015 (New Zealand Emissions Trading Register, 2018[3]); [2]except if certain eligibility criteria apply (see RGGI (2008[4]) for detail.

A.2. Permit prices and ETS coverage

Table A.2 shows the shares of emissions covered by ETS and tradeable performance standards across sectors for all countries and regions included in this report in which emitters could trade permits in 2015. For subnational trading systems, the emissions covered by the ETS and tradeable performance standards are given as shares of national emissions. The last column lists the price of tradeable emission permits in 2015 EUR per tonne of CO_2.

Table A.2. Permit prices and ETS coverage

			ETS coverage						ETS Permit Price (in EUR per tonne of CO_2)
			Road	Off-road	Industrial production	Agriculture & fishing	Residential & Commercial	Electricity	
AUT		Emissions covered by ETS (%)	0%	11%	30%	0%	0%	66%	7.60
BEL		Emissions covered by ETS (%)	0%	1%	53%	0%	0%	69%	7.60
CAN	Alberta	Emissions covered by ETS (%)	0%	9%	33%	0%	0%	54%	10.57
	Quebec	Emissions covered by ETS (%)	15%	6%	6%	7%	9%	0%	11.19
CHE		Emissions covered by ETS (%)	0%	15%	24%	0%	0%	0%	10.95
CHN	Beijing	Emissions covered by ETS (%)	0.0%	0.0%	0.5%	0.0%	0.7%	0.6%	6.05
	Chongqing	Emissions covered by ETS (%)	0.0%	0.0%	1.5%	0.0%	0.0%	0.9%	3.58
	Guangdong	Emissions covered by ETS (%)	0.0%	0.0%	2.7%	0.0%	0.0%	5.6%	2.37
	Hubei	Emissions covered by ETS (%)	0.0%	0.0%	2.0%	0.0%	0.0%	1.9%	3.60
	Shanghai	Emissions covered by ETS (%)	0.0%	0.0%	1.4%	0.0%	3.7%	2.4%	3.42
	Shenzhen	Emissions covered by ETS (%)	0.0%	0.0%	0.0%	0.0%	0.0%	0.6%	5.44
	Tianjin	Emissions covered by ETS (%)	0.0%	0.0%	2.1%	0.0%	0.0%	1.2%	3.19
CZE		Emissions covered by ETS (%)	0%	24%	40%	0%	0%	96%	7.60
DNK		Emissions covered by ETS (%)	0%	10%	51%	2%	0%	73%	7.60
EST		Emissions covered by ETS (%)	0%	0%	33%	0%	0%	88%	7.60
FIN		Emissions covered by ETS (%)	0%	26%	29%	0%	0%	70%	7.60
FRA		Emissions covered by ETS (%)	0%	60%	64%	0%	1%	91%	7.60
DEU		Emissions covered by ETS (%)	0%	41%	64%	0%	0%	90%	7.60
GRC		Emissions covered by ETS (%)	0%	21%	100%	6%	0%	99%	7.60
HUN		Emissions covered by ETS (%)	0%	21%	51%	0%	0%	78%	7.60
ISL		Emissions covered by ETS (%)	0%	45%	4%	0%	0%	0%	7.60
IRL		Emissions covered by ETS (%)	0%	9%	65%	0%	0%	97%	7.60
ITA		Emissions covered by ETS (%)	0%	45%	68%	0%	0%	88%	7.60
JAP	Tokyo	Emissions covered by ETS (%)	0%	0%	0.3%	0%	1.7%	1.9%	9.83
	Saitama	Emissions covered by ETS (%)	0%	0%	3.3%	1.6%	0%	2.2%	9.83
KOR		Emissions covered by ETS (%)	0%	37%	96%	0%	25%	98%	8.95
LUX		Emissions covered by ETS (%)	0%	0%	73%	0%	0%	64%	7.60
NLD		Emissions covered by ETS (%)	0%	3%	63%	8%	1%	97%	7.60
NOR		Emissions covered by ETS (%)	0%	35%	100%	0%	1%	66%	7.60
NZL		Emissions covered by ETS (%)	79%	79%	49%	76%	61%	82%	2.12
POL		Emissions covered by ETS (%)	0%	74%	74%	0%	0%	94%	7.60
PRT		Emissions covered by ETS (%)	0%	51%	42%	0%	0%	93%	7.60
SVK		Emissions covered by ETS (%)	0%	59%	41%	0%	0%	85%	7.60
SVN		Emissions covered by ETS (%)	0%	7%	53%	0%	0%	98%	7.60
ESP		Emissions covered by ETS (%)	0%	73%	62%	0%	1%	95%	7.60
SWE		Emissions covered by ETS (%)	0%	63%	28%	0%	0%	30%	7.60
GBR		Emissions covered by ETS (%)	0%	38%	53%	3%	1%	87%	7.60
USA	California	Emissions covered by ETS (%)	9%	3%	7%	6%	5%	4%	12.44
	RGGI	Emissions covered by ETS (%)	0%	0%	0.1%	0%	0%	4%	6.11

A.3. ETS-specific adjustments and assumptions

Results presented in Table A.2 are based on the general estimation methodology described in OECD (2016[5]). In addition, the following specific adjustments and assumptions apply for the different emissions trading systems.

A.3.1. Canada

Canada prices carbon emissions through tradeable permits at the Provincial level. In 2015, the Quebec Cap-and-Trade System and the Alberta Specified Gas Emitters Regulation, put a price on carbon emissions through tradeable permits.

A.3.1.1. Alberta

Verified emissions for the Alberta Specified Gas Emitters Regulation, a tradeable performance standard, were not available for 2015 at the time of writing. Hence, emission coverage is estimated using 2015 facility-level data on greenhouse gas emissions, differentiated by gas, as published by the Government of Canada (2017[6]). Based on this data, the following system-specific adjustments and assumptions are made:

- The *matching* of facilities to the six Effective Carbon Rate (ECR) sectors is based on the North American Industry Classification System (NAICS) as reported in the dataset (Government of Canada, 2017[6]).

- *Process emissions* are excluded using data from the Canadian Greenhouse Gas Emissions Inventory (Environment Canada, 2017[7]).

- The *price* associated with the Specified Gas Emitters Regulation (SGER) for 2015 is assumed to be CAD 15 per tonne CO_2, which corresponds to the permit price emitters had to pay to Alberta's Climate Change and Emissions Management Fund for compliance obligations they could not meet in a more cost-effective way (make improvements at their facility to reduce emissions; use emission performance credits generated at facilities that achieve more than the required reductions; purchase Alberta-based carbon offset credits).

A.3.1.4. Quebec

Data on emissions subject to the Quebec Cap-and-Trade System in 2015 is from Quebec's Ministry of Sustainable Development, Environment and the Fight against Climate Change (Gouvernement du Québec, 2017[8]). The dataset reports the verified greenhouse gas emissions in 2015 of all facilities and fuel suppliers subject to the system. In addition, the following ETS-specific adjustments and assumptions are made:

- *Matching* of facilities to the six sectors discussed in the main body of the report is based on the North American Industry Classification System (NAICS) as in the previous edition of Effective Carbon Rates (OECD, 2016[5]).

- *Non-CO_2 emissions* are removed based on facility-reported emissions data, which is differentiated by gas (Government of Canada, 2017[6]).

- *Process emissions* are excluded and *fuel suppliers* included combining the verified emissions dataset with provincial-level data contained in the Canadian Greenhouse Gas Emissions Inventory (Environment Canada, 2017[7]).

- The average auction price in 2015 was CAD 15.88 per tonne of CO_2 (average of four auctions, weighted by the number of allowances sold).

A.3.2. People's Republic of China

The estimation of emissions covered by the Chinese Pilot ETSs follows Li et al. (2015[9]) as outlined in Annex B in OECD (2016[5]). The estimation by Li et al. (2015[9]) follows largely the general estimation methodology as detailed in Annex A in OECD (2016[5]), but deviations occur due to different structures and availability of data. In particular, the following specific adjustments to the general estimation methodology and assumptions are made:

- *Industrial process emissions* from lime and cement production are excluded from the estimation of the emissions trading systems in Beijing, Chongqing, Guangdong, Shanghai and Shenzhen using a uniform process emission factor (0.57 tonnes CO_2 per tonne of cement) from the literature. Cement and lime production account for 87% of China's total industrial process emissions in 2005 (UNFCCC, 2015[10]).

- *Auto-generation of electricity* in China mainly occurs in the aluminium sector (Li, 2015[11]). Because the vast majority of Chinese aluminium is produced outside the area of the seven pilot systems, no adjustment for auto-electricity is made.

- To calculate *indirect CO_2 emissions from electricity*, an average value for the national carbon intensity of electricity production is used. This implicitly assumes that electricity consumed in different sectors and regions is produced based on the same energy mix.

- In *Shanghai*, emissions from air transport subject to the ETS are currently allocated to the commercial and residential sector.

- In *Shenzhen*, 197 public buildings are covered by the Shenzhen ETS, but no information is available to estimate the total sector coverage.

- Prices:
    - Beijing's average price in 2015 amounts to CNY 41.70 (EUR 6.05) per tonne CO2
    - Chongqing's average price in 2015 amounts to CNY 24.75 (EUR 3.58) per tonne CO_2
    - Guangdong's average price in 2015 amounts to CNY 16.38 (EUR 2.37) per tonne CO_2
    - Hubei's average price in 2015 amounts to CNY 24.84 (EUR 3.60) per tonne CO_2
    - Shanghai's average price in 2015 amounts to CNY 23.65 (EUR 3.42) per tonne CO_2
    - Shenzhen's average price in 2015 amounts to CNY 37.55 (EUR 5.44) per tonne CO_2
    - Tianjin's average price in 2015 amounts to CNY 22.02 (EUR 3.19) per tonne CO_2

- To determine the price signal sent by ETS in China, an average price from all pilot systems was calculated for each sector, weighted by the proportion of covered emissions from each system in that sector. Price information is based on market prices from the emission exchanges in 2015, see PMR (2015[12]), PMR (2015[13]), and PMR (2015[14]).

- The weighted effective average *price* in China amounts to CNY 22.82 (EUR 3.30) in the industry sector, CNY 26.71 (i.e. EUR 3.87) in the commercial and residential sector, CNY 22.08 (i.e. EUR 3.20) in the electricity sector.[1]

A.3.3. EU

Data on verified emissions from more than 11 000 installations, and their corresponding economic activity classification, is from the European Commission (2017[15]). In addition, the following specific assumptions are made:

- The Statistical Classification of Economic Activities in the European Community (NACE) classifies economic activities into 615 economic classes. Where available, NACE codes are used to *match* emissions from installations to Effective Carbon Rate (ECR) sectors.[2] If no NACE code is available installations are matched to ECR sectors codes using a compulsory activity code, that derives from the list of activities included in the EU ETS shown above. For electricity generation and heat generation installations, there is only one common activity code. To distinguish between emissions from electricity and heat generation from installations with no NACE code but a common activity code two steps are undertaken. First, a ratio of emissions from electricity generation installations to heat generation installations is built based on information from installations for which a NACE code is available. Second emissions from electricity and heat generation from installations with no NACE code but a common activity code, are attributed to electricity and heat generation according to the ratio calculated in the first step.

- The *electricity sector* is covered at close to 100% in most countries, given that even small fossil fuel power plants (>= 20 MW capacity) have to take part in the ETS. For some countries coverage was initially estimated to exceed 100% in the electricity sector. This is a consequence of initially allocating all emissions from electricity generation under the ETS to the electricity sector, even though some of these emissions result from auto-electricity generation in the industry sector. NACE and activity codes only specify the main activity of an installation. A power plant owned by an industrial company that produces electricity for its own production, but at the same time also for the grid maybe coded simply as a power plant. All its emissions would then be coded as emissions from the electricity sector, even though some are from auto-electricity generation in the industry sector. Knowing that the coverage of the electricity sector cannot be above 100% and that the rules on inclusion of power plants onto the ETS imply close to 100% coverage of the electricity sector any emissions in excess of 100% coverage of the electricity sector are called overflow emissions and separated from the electricity sector. These overflow emissions are then allocated to the industry sector, given that they result from auto-generation of electricity in the industry sector.

- With respect to *aviation*, commercial flights within the EEA area are covered by the EU ETS as described above. The Taxing Energy Use database only takes emission from domestic flights into account. For that reasons it is assumed that all regularly scheduled domestic flights are covered by the EU ETS, which are 97%

of all flights within the EEA according to a study for the European Aviation Safety Agency (EASA, 2009[16]).

- The average allowance *price* of all auctions in 2015 was EUR 7.60 per tonne of CO_2 (European Energy Exchange, 2015[17]).

A.3.4. Japan

A.3.4.1. Tokyo

Emissions by sector from are from the Tokyo Metropolitan Government (TMG, 2017[18]). In addition, the following country-specific assumptions are made:

- The share of *indirect emissions from electricity use*, i.e. emission from electricity bought from an electricity provider, in total emissions is calculated for each sector using Tokyo's greenhouse gas inventory (TMG, 2017[19]). Thereby it is assumed that the share of indirect emissions from electricity use in total emissions is the same for covered and non-covered facilities in a given sector.

- 2015 emissions under the cap are currently not available by economic subsector. For this reason subsector data from the latest year available, i.e. 2010, are *scaled* to 2015 by the difference of aggregate emissions under the cap from 2010 to 2015.

- The detailed subsector data for 2010 has only been published as preliminary data. Meanwhile official data show higher aggregate emissions for 2010 than the preliminary data does. The preliminary by subsector data is therefore *scaled* to match the official aggregate data for 2010.

- According to Jin (2017[20]) one excess reduction credit traded between JPY 1080 and JPY 1550. One excess reduction credit allows emitting one tonne CO_2 (TMG, 2012[21]). For the calculation of effective carbon rates a central estimate of JPY 1320 per tonne CO_2 for 2015 is assumed.

A.3.4.2 Saitama

Emissions by sector from are from the Saitama Prefectural Government (SPG, 2017[22]). In addition, the following country-specific assumptions are made:

- The share of *indirect emissions from electricity use*, i.e. emission from electricity bought from an electricity provider, in total emissions is calculated for each sector using Saitama's greenhouse gas inventory (SPG, 2017[23]). Thereby it is assumed that the share of indirect emissions from electricity use in total emissions is the same for covered and non-covered facilities for a given sector.

- The Saitama ETS is linked with the Tokyo ETS via SME credits. Therefore it is assumed that the credit price from Tokyo also applies to Saitama. According to Jin (2017[20]) one excess reduction credit traded between JPY 1080 and JPY 1550. One excess reduction credit allows emitting one tonne CO_2 (TMG, 2012[21]). For the calculation of effective carbon rates a central estimate of JPY 1320 per tonne CO_2 for 2015 is assumed.

A.3.5. Korea

The Korean Ministry of Environment provided aggregated sector data on verified carbon dioxide emissions covered by the Korean emissions trading system in 2015. In addition, the following ETS-specific assumptions and adjustments are made:

- *Industrial process emissions* are retrieved from the UNFCCC as submitted by the Korean authorities.

- *Non-GHG emissions* had been excluded from the aggregated data provided by the Ministry of Environment. Hence no adjustment for non-GHG emissions was necessary.

- It is assumed that *biomass* is covered by the system, but that its emissions factor is equal to zero.

- The average permit *price* was KRW 11230 per tonne of CO_2 in 2015 according to data provided by the Korean Ministry of Environment.

A.3.6. New Zealand

The coverage of the New Zealand ETS is estimated differently than for the other ETS. Given that the New Zealand ETS is an upstream ETS, applying to fuels (whether imported or produced) rather than to users, coverage is estimated by calculating which proportion of each fuel type is subject to the ETS. The proportion of ETS coverage for emissions from each fuel is assumed to apply uniformly to all users of that fuel. To calculate coverage at the user level, total covered emissions from fuels used by each user are then divided by the total emissions for that user. Data on total covered emissions by user by calendar year are published by the New Zealand Environmental Protection Agency. In addition, the following assumptions are made:

- CO_2 *emissions occur* from energy use occur *primarily through liquid fossil fuel combustion and in the stationary energy sector*. Consequently, non-energy related emissions (e.g. industrial processes or agriculture) have been excluded from the estimation.

- The data retrieved from the New Zealand Environmental Protection Agency lists *emissions from industrial processes* separately from emissions from energy use, allowing exclusion of industrial process emissions from the estimation.

- It is assumed that ETS participants fully pass ETS costs on to end users.

- The average *price* of New Zealand Units (NZUs) is used, to reflect the fact that 97% of surrendered permits in 2015 were NZUs (49% Forestry NZUs; 48% Other NZUs) (New Zealand Environmental Protection Agency, 2015[24]). From 1 June 2015, only NZUs and New Zealand-based assigned amount units (NZAAUs) are eligible to meet the NZ ETS obligations (New Zealand Ministry for the Environment, 2016[25]).

- The rate of permits is halved because one permit is surrendered for every two tonnes of CO_2 emissions. The average permit price has been calculated as half the average NZU price for 2015: EUR 2.12 per tonne CO_2, or NZD 3.38 per tonne CO_2 (Carbonnews, 2018[26]). This one-for-two transition measure is gradually phased out over three years starting January 1, 2017 (New Zealand Ministry for the Environment, 2016[27]).

ANNEX A. DESCRIPTION OF EMISSIONS TRADING SYSTEMS AND RESULTS | 87

A.3.7. Switzerland

A list of ETS installations, as well as surrendered emissions by facility and year, are taken from the website of the Swiss Emissions Trading Registry (2018[28]). Covered facilities are matched to sectors based on information provided by Swiss Federal Office for the Environment for the previous edition of this report (OECD, 2016[5]). In addition, the following country-specific adjustments and assumptions are made:

- Installation-level data on non-CO_2 emission are retrieved from the Swiss Pollutant Registry (Swiss Federal Office for the Environment, 2017[29]) and deducted from verified ETS emissions.

- *Process emissions* as declared by Switzerland to the UNFCCC (Swiss Federal Office for the Environment, 2017[30]) are deducted from the industry sectors with process emissions.

- The weighted average of the three allowance auctions of 2015 is applied as the permit *price*.

- The 2015 emission permit *price* amounts to CHF 11.68 per tonne of CO_2.

A.3.8. USA

To determine the price signal sent by emissions trading systems in the USA an average auction price from RGGI and the California system was calculated for all sectors, weighted by the proportion of emissions subject to each system in that sector.

The weighted average auction price in the USA in 2015 amounts to USD 12.33 in the industry sector, USD 9.07 in electricity and USD 12.44 in all other sectors.

A.3.8.1. RGGI

Data on verified emissions of facilities covered by system is obtained from RGGI reports on annual emissions (RGGI, 2017[31]). In addition, the following system-specific adjustments and assumptions are made:

- All emissions are *attributed to the main industrial sector* of the facility as specified by the North American Industry Classification System (NAICS). The NAICS codes of all facilities is obtained from the Energy Information Agency (EIA, 2017[32]).

- The average auction clearing *price* in 2015 was USD 6.11 per tonne CO_2 (RGGI, 2017[33]).

A.3.8.2. California

Data on greenhouse gas emissions subject to a compliance obligation in the Cap-and-Trade Program are published at the facility level by the Californian Air Resource Board (ARB) in the "Annual Summary of GHG Mandatory Reporting" (California ARB, 2017[34]). Based on this data the following system-specific adjustments and assumptions are made:

- The *matching* of facilities to the six Effective Carbon Rate (ECR) sectors is based on the North American Industry Classification System (NAICS). NAICS codes are reported for all facilities in California ARB (2017[34]). In specific cases, activity codes, as reported in California ARB, (2017[34]), have been used to refine the match.

- Emissions from *fuel suppliers* have been attributed to the six sectors based on the following main assumptions: first, the transport sector is fully covered from transportation fuel suppliers, and second, the remaining fuel supplier emissions are allocated to all other sectors at a constant share.
- *Non-CO_2 and industrial process emissions* are excluded based on information from the California Greenhouse Gas Emission Inventory (California ARB, 2017[35]).
- The average auction *price* in 2015 was USD 12.44 per tonne CO_2 (California ARB, 2017[36]).

Notes

[1] Exchange rates are from the OECD.Stat database (OECD, 2017[94]).

[2] Sector definitions used in this report and outlined in Section A.1.3 of OECD (2016[3]) do not always match sector categories applied by individual countries.

References

California ARB (2017), *California Cap and Trade Program – Summary of Joint Auction Settlement Prices and Results*, https://www.arb.ca.gov/cc/capandtrade/auction/results_summary.pdf (accessed on 08 December 2017). [36]

California ARB (2017), *California's Greenhouse Gas Inventory by IPCC Category*, https://www.arb.ca.gov/cc/inventory/data/tables/ghg_inventory_by_ipcc_all_00-15.xlsx (accessed on 15 December 2017). [35]

California ARB (2017), *GHG Data - California Air Resources Board - State of California*, https://www.arb.ca.gov/cc/reporting/ghg-rep/reported-data/2015-ghg-emissions-2017-11-06.xlsx (accessed on 06 December 2017). [34]

Carbonnews (2018), *OMF NZ Market Report Archive*, http://www.carbonnews.co.nz/tagarchive.asp?tag=OMF+NZ+Market+Report (accessed on 27 March 2018). [26]

EASA (2009), *SAVE - Study on Aviation and Economic Modelling, Final Report*, European Aviation Safety Agency, Cologne. [16]

EIA (2017), *Form EIA-860 detailed data for 2015*, http://www.eia.gov/electricity/data/eia860/ (accessed on 18 December 2017). [32]

Environment Canada (2017), *National Inventory Report 1990-2015: Greenhouse Gas Sources and Sinks in Canada*, http://donnees.ec.gc.ca/data/substances/monitor/national-and-provincial-territorial-greenhouse-gas-emission-tables/?l. [7]

European Commission (2017), *Union Registry: Compliance data for 2016*, European Commission, Brussels, https://ec.europa.eu/clima/policies/ets/registry_en#tab-0-1 (accessed on 23 March 2018). [15]

European Energy Exchange (2015), *Emission Spot Primary Market Auction Report 2015*, European Energy Exchange, Leipzig, https://www.eex.com/de/marktdaten/umweltprodukte/auktionsmarkt/european-emission-allowances-auction/european-emission-allowances-auction-download (accessed on 23 March 2018). [17]

Gouvernement du Québec (2017), *Émissions de gaz à effet de serre déclarées et vérifiées des établissements visés par le RSPEDE*, http://www.mddelcc.gouv.qc.ca/changements/carbone/documentation.htm. [8]

Gouvernement du Québec (2017), "Regulation respecting a cap-and-trade system for greenhouse gas emission allowances". [1]

Government of Canada (2017), *Facility-reported greenhouse gas data*, https://www.canada.ca/en/environment-climate-change/services/climate-change/greenhouse-gas-emissions/facility-reporting/data.html. [6]

Jin, Z. (2017), *Current Status of Emission Trading Schemes (ETSs) in Japan, China and South Korea*, Presentation at ISAP 2017. [20]

Li, J. (2015), *Integrating Cap and Trade into Taxing Energy Use: Interim Report for China*, report prepared for the OECD. [9]

Li, J. (2015), *Personal Communication*. [11]

New Zealand Emissions Trading Register (2018), *Public information and reports*, https://www.eur.govt.nz/Authentication/Logon.aspx?ReturnUrl=%2fdefault.aspx (accessed on 27 March 2018). [3]

New Zealand Environmental Protection Agency (2015), *Facts and figures 2015*. [24]

New Zealand Ministry for the Environment (2016), *Phase out of the one-for-two transitional measure from the New Zealand Emissions Trading Scheme*. [27]

New Zealand Ministry for the Environment (2016), *The New Zealand Emissions Trading Scheme Evaluation 2016*, http://www.mfe.govt.nz.. [25]

OECD (2016), *Effective Carbon Rates: Pricing CO2 through Taxes and Emissions Trading Systems*, OECD Publishing, Paris, http://dx.doi.org/10.1787/9789264260115-en. [5]

PMR (2015), "China Carbon Market Monitor", *The PMR China Carbon Market Monitor* 1. [12]

PMR (2015), "China Carbon Market Monitor", *The PMR China Carbon Market Monitor* 2. [13]

PMR (2015), "China Carbon Market Monitor", *The PMR China Carbon Market Monitor* 3. [14]

RGGI (2017), *Reports: Annual Emissions – Facility Level View*, https://rggi-coats.org/eats/rggi/index.cfm?hc=ISkwICAK (accessed on 18 December 2017). [31]

RGGI (2017), *Transaction Price Report*, https://rggi-coats.org/eats/rggi/index.cfm?hc=ISkwICAK (accessed on 18 December 2017). [33]

RGGI (2008), *Regional greenhouse gas initiative model rule: 12/31/08 with corrections,*, Regional Greenhouse Gas Initiative, New York. [4]

SPG (2017), *Saitama 2015 Emission Data*, http://www.pref.saitama.lg.jp/a0502/sakugen.html (accessed on 31 January 2018). [22]

SPG (2017), *Saitama Prefecture Greenhouse Gas Emission Inventory 2015*, Saitama Prefecture Environment Department, Saitama. [23]

Swiss Emissions Trading Registry (2018), *Public information*, https://www.emissionsregistry.admin.ch. [28]

Swiss Federal Council (2012), *Ordinance on the Reduction of CO2 Emissions*. [2]

Swiss Federal Office for the Environment (2017), *Swiss Pollutant Release and Transfer Register*, http://www.ubst.bafu.admin.ch/opendata/UBD0001.ods. [29]

Swiss Federal Office for the Environment (2017), "Switzerland's Greenhouse Gas Inventory 1990–2015", https://www.bafu.admin.ch/dam/bafu/en/dokumente/klima/klima-climatereporting/switzerland_s_most_recent_national_inventory_report.pdf.download.pdf/Switzerland's%20National%20Inventory%20Report%202017%20(GHG%20inventory%201990-2015).pdf. [30]

TMG (2017), *Final Energy Consumption and Greenhouse Gas Emissions in Tokyo*, Tokyo Muncipal Government, Bureau of Environment. [19]

TMG (2017), *Results of the Tokyo Cap-and-Trade Program for the First Fiscal Year of Second Compliance Period*, Tokyo Municipal Government, Bureau of Environment. [18]

TMG (2012), *Total reduction obligations and emissions trading scheme. Assessment of transaction prices.*, Tokyo Municipal Government, Bureau of Environment. [21]

UNFCCC (2015), *Submitted National Communications from non-Annex I Parties: Second National Communication on Climate Change of The People's Republic of China*, http://unfccc.int/resource/docs/natc/chnnc2e.pdf (accessed on 06 October 2015). [10]

ORGANISATION FOR ECONOMIC CO-OPERATION AND DEVELOPMENT

The OECD is a unique forum where governments work together to address the economic, social and environmental challenges of globalisation. The OECD is also at the forefront of efforts to understand and to help governments respond to new developments and concerns, such as corporate governance, the information economy and the challenges of an ageing population. The Organisation provides a setting where governments can compare policy experiences, seek answers to common problems, identify good practice and work to co-ordinate domestic and international policies.

The OECD member countries are: Australia, Austria, Belgium, Canada, Chile, the Czech Republic, Denmark, Estonia, Finland, France, Germany, Greece, Hungary, Iceland, Ireland, Israel, Italy, Japan, Korea, Latvia, Lithuania, Luxembourg, Mexico, the Netherlands, New Zealand, Norway, Poland, Portugal, the Slovak Republic, Slovenia, Spain, Sweden, Switzerland, Turkey, the United Kingdom and the United States. The European Union takes part in the work of the OECD.

OECD Publishing disseminates widely the results of the Organisation's statistics gathering and research on economic, social and environmental issues, as well as the conventions, guidelines and standards agreed by its members.

www.ingramcontent.com/pod-product-compliance
Lightning Source LLC
Chambersburg PA
CBHW082353220526
45470CB00008B/2727